Developing Successful Marketing Strategies

Developing Successful Marketing Strategies

Gary W. Randazzo

First published in 2014 by
Business Expert Press, LLC
222 East 46th Street, New York, NY 10017
www.businessexpertpress.com

ISBN-13: 978-1-60649-960-3 (paperback)
ISBN-13: 978-1-60649-961-0 (e-book)

Business Expert Press Marketing Strategy Collection

Collection ISSN: 2150-9654 (print)
Collection ISSN: 2150-9662 (electronic)

Cover and interior design by Exeter Premedia Services Private Ltd., Chennai, India

First edition: 2014

10 9 8 7 6 5 4 3 2 1

Printed in the United States of America.

Abstract

Developing Successful Marketing Strategies uses real market examples to demonstrate the development of effective marketing strategies. The approach uses an organization's mission and vision statements to guide the development of marketing goals, strategies, and tactics.

Central to the development of marketing strategy is the use of the marketing mix of price, place, product, and promotion. The book neatly weaves the process of developing a marketing strategy with the use of the marketing mix. Throughout the book examples are given to clarify the theories and guide the reader through the strategic marketing planning process.

Managers and executives will use this book as a guide to grow an established business or start a new one. The book can be used as a reference book for unique marketing challenges as well.

The book differs from other business books in that it introduces management techniques and processes and shows how they are critical to executing successful marketing strategies.

The examples used in *Developing Successful Marketing Strategies* are from large and small organizations in which the author was personally involved. The techniques introduced in the book are based on those studied at most universities.

Keywords

advertising frequency, cash requirements, consumer adoption drivers, cross functional teams, customer categories, execution management, mission, new product development, objective, organizational structure, vision, place, price, product, promotion, situation analysis, strategy, tactics, workforce

Contents

Preface

Building a successful marketing strategy is like taking a road trip. You have to know where you want to go, what you want the experience to be like, and you have to know the starting point. Once the starting and ending points have been identified, designing the trip according to expectations becomes a lot easier. The trip's outcome is more easily determined if the planning includes a look at the resources required, the exact route, and possible complications from outside forces such as the weather or traffic congestion.

A vision and mission statement usually identifies the desired destination. The vision and mission statement defines what you want to accomplish and sets the parameters for how your organization will operate.

If the vision and mission statement is too vague, it will be difficult to create a plan that will result in a clear direction for the enterprise. Similarly, too much detail in a vision and mission statement can limit the success of the enterprise.

In Houston, I work with a group of academicians and clinicians who are focused on creating a research institute to develop devices to deliver health care to underserved populations affordably.

The following is a proposed mission and vision statement:

eHealth Research Institute Mission and Vision Statement

Mission:

- To make available quality, affordable health care to all individuals worldwide
- To provide barrier breaking solutions to obstacles impeding the delivery of health care through the use of technology and telecommunications
- To create value and make a difference

Vision: To create a collaborative network of clinicians, researchers, academicians, and partners focused on creating modes of delivering affordable health care worldwide. This will be accomplished by

- attracting the best and brightest people to work in an environment that is challenging and rewarding;
- creating a network of technology and industrial partners that is focused on innovative solutions to health care delivery;
- establishing a center in Houston that serves as the worldwide center and incubator for telehealth care solutions;
- working with hospitals and medical institutions worldwide to deploy new medical delivery innovations by technology and through telecommunications;
- working with industrial and financial partners to create new markets for telehealth care delivery solutions;
- developing an organization that is highly effective, lean, and fast moving;
- maximizing long-term financial return for partners and long-term sustainability for the eHealth Research Institute (Randazzo 2013, 3–4).

This mission and vision statement provides a framework that can be used to build a plan for the organization. Based on the aforementioned, it is apparent that the research institute will provide a place where physicians, engineers, academicians, and participants from industry can work together to develop products that can be commercialized. From here a planning group can begin designing the organization and start estimating resources that will be needed. They will also be able to identify activities that are required to put the organization into place.

Developing a Marketing Strategy

In designing a marketing strategy for a business, understanding the starting point is critical and requires a very detailed description. This description will include market forces and situations that are internal and external to the organization. It should include resources available and potential challenges.

After the starting point or the current state of affairs for the organization is understood, then the objective (this is driven by the vision and mission statement) to be achieved can be stated. The more clearly the objective is stated, the better the chance that any marketing strategy that is developed will be focused on achieving the objective.

After the objective is identified, then development of the marketing strategy can begin. The strategy will recognize how each of the four Ps of marketing will be used to reach the objective.

After the strategy is developed, the real work of creating a tactical plan to successfully execute the strategy must be developed. The tactical plan outlines the tactics for each of the four Ps and describes in detail how the firm's resources will be utilized and impacted.

The discussion that follows offers a simple example of how strategy, tactics, and the four Ps of marketing work together.

Assess the Current Situation

Before the development of a marketing strategy, it is important to assess the environment in which the organization will operate. This analysis will identify the nature of the industry, the market, the competition, resources available, and other factors that will determine the direction, magnitude, and objectives for the marketing strategy. Once the environment has been assessed, then the strategist can begin considering marketing objectives.

Set an Objective

The marketing effort begins with an objective. This objective can be to create a new business to serve a specific market, launch a new product for an existing business, develop a new market with existing products, and so on.

After establishing the objective, it is important to take a hard look at the business you are in or are hoping to start. This exercise will help to better understand your current position in the industry and possible avenues for growth. For example, if owning a cupcake specialty shop, you should determine whether you are in the cupcake business, confectionary business, restaurant business, or bakery business, and so on. The choice will affect the strategy that might be employed to achieve the objective.

Identify a Customer Base

Also considering the business, it is important to identify the potential customer base (key customers) you will be serving and your business capabilities. For example, if you are entering an established market but have limited resources, you may be forced to serve the least profitable customer. In other words, the market leaders will have developed products and services that serve the most profitable customers and your limited resources will put you at a disadvantage when competing for those customers.

This exercise may also uncover other customer segments that may offer opportunities but may not represent the key customer category. If you, for example, served the least profitable customer you might also find some of the industry's more profitable customers have a reason to choose your product or service.

Going after the least profitable customers may be an advantage since the market leaders are not likely to focus on customers who would require resources to be taken from efforts to serve their more profitable clients. This approach would make you a disruptor and your product a disruptive innovation since you would be starting with the least profitable customer and work to create ways to "move up the customer chain" in this market.

On the other hand, if you have a new idea or innovation and want to compete for the very profitable customers, then you must consider ways of protecting your market position. Since this innovation can likely be duplicated in some fashion by the competition, it will be important to choose a marketing strategy that makes duplication by competitors more difficult.

Set a Strategy

Strategy is *what* you will do to reach your objective that is driven by your vision and mission statement.

As an example, let's say that your objective is to become a leader in providing exterior maintenance service. If, in the beginning, you had some basic equipment and could perform basic pressure washing of concrete, you might decide to start a business to clean concrete surfaces. Your customers would likely be individuals who could not afford or perhaps didn't need the range of services offered by the more established pressure washing services. A careful look at the type of business, the customer segment, and the resources might be helpful in developing a marketing strategy. In this case, the strategic statement (the *what* you want to do) might be: "To enter the maintenance service business by providing basic pressure washing services to homeowners with a plan to expand service offerings to homeowners and businesses in Texas."

In this case, you are a potential market disruptor (trying to make a profit serving the least profitable customer) that will be part of the maintenance service industry and will start with a pressure washing service.

Develop the Tactics

Tactics are *how* you will successfully execute the strategy.

Tactics will require attention to the price, place, product, and promotion components of marketing and the planning, organizing, directing, and controlling principles of management. Additionally, the tactics will have to consider how the marketing components and management principles fit with the workforce, financial requirements and capabilities, capital equipment needs, and operational procedures.

The more the marketing, management, and operational plans are in concert, the better the chances of achieving the strategic goal. This set of exercises is critical in the sense that they are focused on creating the most efficient, objective driven organization possible.

Considering the pressure washing service, the tactics might involve the following:

1. **Product**: Begin with power washing home decks, driveways, and sidewalks; expanding to gutter cleaning, window cleaning, and pool service; then moving into commercial maintenance (this approach provides the ability to grow horizontally and vertically—gateway capacity).

2. **Pricing**: Start with simple low-level pricing moving to a bundling approach as more services are added. This allows the ability to sell new services to existing customers and create customer loyalty by

providing discounts based on the number of services purchased. Additionally, contract pricing would be provided for long-term purchase commitments.

3. **Place**: Begin in an area easily served by limited manpower and resources with a plan to expand to adjacent areas so that supply chain and resources are not strained.

4. **Promotion**: Limit promotion to grow business within the ability to serve the demand. Begin with very targeted, low-cost promotion and expand as territory is increased.

5. **Workforce**: Contract labor that can be quickly assigned to complete jobs. As the business grows, evaluate the need for permanent employees with specialized expertise.

6. **Financial requirements**: A small amount of start-up cash and initial payment from customers should be enough to cover the cost of completing the job. Consider half payment at sale and half at completion. Put aside 20 percent of each job for investment into company growth and new equipment. Assume 10 percent of each job will be used for repair and maintenance.

7. **Operational procedures**: Utilize contract labor at negotiated and contracted rates that allow easy determination and maintenance of profit margins. Require bonding of contractors to provide assurance that the job will be completed and allow some level of comfort to the customer when requiring half of the job cost be paid in advance.

8. **Capital equipment**: Lease basic, rugged pressure washing equipment in the beginning. Consider purchasing equipment when it is advantageous. Expand the inventory of equipment as business increases.

This is a simple example but illustrates that there is a sequence that should be followed for the best results. If you start with tactical measures or with a strategy that hasn't identified the industry or customer base, a great deal of time will be spent on course correcting to develop a successful model.

Every time you re-evaluate and change direction, internal changes are required that can be costly in that each of the previously listed tactical categories will likely be impacted.

This process works for established businesses, new businesses, and businesses that have had a significant change in their industry.

Simply stated: "Vision and mission statement before objective, objective before strategy, and strategy before tactics."

This book is based on the premise that the four Ps of marketing (price, place, product, and promotion) must be used in concert to develop a successful marketing strategy. Further, the strategy must work within the market constraints and challenges and within the firm's resources to reach the overall marketing objectives.

The material that is presented is designed to provide managers with a structured approach that can be used to develop a successful marketing strategy for any organization.

PART I

Situation Analysis

The situation analysis is the first step in developing a marketing strategy. A situation analysis is a gathering of data that details the current state of an organization and its environment. Much like planning a trip, the situation analysis identifies the starting point and the conditions that exist at the beginning of the trip. For a trip it is important to know the mode of transportation, the condition of the infrastructure along which the transportation moves, the amount of fuel and other resources available, and so on.

For organizations developing a marketing strategy, the situation analysis begins with the industry, the market, and the competition.

CHAPTER 1

Industry and Market

When developing an assessment of the market and the industry, it is important to take a macroview of the market and identify the job that consumers need done. This chapter focuses on information that is needed on the industry and the market in which a company plans to focus its strategic marketing efforts.

Theodore Levitt's seminal work on marketing myopia stated that railroads were not in trouble in the 1970s because the need for moving people and products had diminished. Railroads were in trouble because they viewed themselves as being in the railroad business instead of being in the transportation business.

Using Clayton Christensen's theories on disruptive innovation, new forms of transporting people and products were not a disruptive innovation focused on providing the railroad's least profitable customers with a "good enough" product. Rather, these new forms of transportation were a sustaining technology that would have allowed railroad industry leaders the ability to better serve their most profitable customers.

In this case, we are suggesting that railroads are in the transportation business, and the ability to provide transportation services to augment railroad delivery might be an option to consider when developing a strategy. Clearly if the industry focus is too narrow, some options will not be considered.

The same is true of identifying the potential market. If a marketing strategist defines the market too narrowly, potential customers will be overlooked. Consider Southwest Airlines, one of the few airlines to consistently show a profit. Clearly they are in the transportation industry but what is their market? Many might say the market is made up of individuals needing airline transportation.

Southwest suggested that the market included airline customers but the focus was on individuals needing transportation for medium range distances. This meant that their market included individuals who could travel by automobile. This dramatically increased the size of the market and redefined the potential parameters of a marketing strategy.

Using Information to Create a Competitive Advantage

Once the strategist is comfortable with the definition of the industry it is necessary to begin studying the market and the potential competitors.

Information on the market and the competition is readily available if you know where to look. Information on the market is available through census data, industry data, and consumer research. Most of this is readily available on the Internet.

Data on the competition is also readily available. Some of the information can be taken from financial reports if the competitor is a publicly traded company. These reports usually give key statistics, profiles of key managers, and basic financial data.

Information on competitors can also be gathered from customers, vendors, and public records. Developing financial profiles of a competitor's business can also provide valuable information.

This information can point to some strengths and weaknesses of the competitors, opportunities and threats in the market place, in the environment, and customer profiles.

Following are a couple of examples that underscore how specific information can be gathered and can help in developing a competitive advantage.

The Houston Post

In late 1994, newspapers were confronted with rapidly rising newsprint costs. I was the Financial Director at the *Houston Chronicle* at the time. We decided that although we had good relationships with suppliers and strong contracts through our parent company, Hearst, it would be important to project future newsprint rate increases and develop advertising and circulation rate increase programs. As a result, the *Chronicle* announced that it would have three 8 percent rate increases: one in September 1994, one in January 1995, and one in June 1995.

We were concerned about our major competitor, the *Houston Post*. They, of course, could decide not to increase their ad or circulation rates and gain market share.

I had been tracking the ad linage each day for the *Houston Post* by purchasing their newspaper and measuring the ads. I estimated their ad rates based on what we learned from customers who bought ads from the *Post*. Making assumptions based on circulation and the size of their organization, I was able to have a pretty good idea of the Post's revenues, expenses, and contribution margin. My projections showed that the *Post* had a small contribution margin and my guess was that they too would increase ad rates for two reasons. First, they would increase ad rates to accommodate the rise in newsprint costs and second, they would increase ad rates because local advertisers wanted two major newspapers competing against each other to hold ad rates down.

One of the interesting things I learned while doing the research was that the *Post* did not have long-term newsprint agreements with the manufacturers and was buying newsprint on the spot commodities market. This meant their newsprint costs would be much more volatile than ours. This made it even more likely that they would increase their ad rates in concert with our announced rate increases.

Unbelievably, the *Post* announced that they would not increase ad rates and the *Chronicle* reports of rising newsprint costs were inaccurate. As soon as this announcement was made, I went to the *Chronicle's* President, Gene McDavid, and said that I could not see the *Post* making it for another six months using that strategy. Clearly newsprint rates were going up and if the *Post* were able to gain more advertising by not raising rates they would require more newsprint at volatile spot market rates.

Interestingly, in April 1995, the *Chronicle* bought the assets of the *Post* and Houston became a major newspaper town.

Creating a pricing strategy for advertising and circulation during this time was dependent upon gathering quality information on the market and the competition. The sources of information had to be reliable. Newsprint rate increase information came from the vendors selling newsprint with which the *Chronicle* had outstanding relationships. Information on the competition came from tracking the competitor as well as newsprint salespeople who let the *Chronicle* know about the buying habits of the competition.

While the *Chronicle* did not anticipate the move made by the *Post* on advertising rates, the approach used by the *Chronicle* set a strategy that would be successful regardless of the actions of the competition.

ADVO

In late 1995, the *Houston Chronicle* embarked on a strategy to recapture advertising revenue lost to direct mail, specifically revenue lost to *marriage mail*.

Marriage mail is a program that allows several advertisers to put their circulars in a mail package and share the postage expense. This provides cost savings to the advertiser. ADVO, a direct mail company that was purchased by Valassis Communications in 2007, became a leader in providing this type of advertising package nationwide. During the 1980s, many retailers moved their circular advertising out of newspapers and into ADVO's marriage mail program.

Houston newspapers lost virtually all of the grocery advertising to ADVO in the mid-1980s. Prior to ADVO, grocery advertising had been a key advertising revenue source for the *Houston Chronicle*.

I led the effort to create a product to compete with the ADVO program. It seemed that the *Chronicle* would be able to combine mail delivery (for non-newspaper subscribers) with newspaper delivery (for newspaper subscribers) and provide an advertising product similar to ADVO's product that would be less expensive, since circulars could be added to newspapers without increasing the delivery costs.

In the information gathering process, we discovered that ADVO earned low postal rates by providing saturation coverage (covering 100 percent of the households). ADVO also saved costs by eliminating the mail labels on each package (each package had the same contents and went to every house, thereby eliminating the need for a label and making delivery very easy for the post office).

We knew that by combining newspaper delivery with mail delivery, we would need to provide each mailed package with an address label since no area would consist of only mail or only newspaper delivery. We also knew that to get the lowest postal rates, we would have to put our mail packages in postal carrier walk sequence to make the delivery for the addressed package as easy as the ADVO package.

Developing a newspaper and labeled mail delivery product for the *Chronicle* advertisers resulted in a program that could provide customized delivery for advertisers. That is, since we knew the addresses of subscribers and mail delivered nonsubscribers, we could have different circulars in each package. For advertisers, this meant that they could have different advertising circulars for different neighborhoods or subdivisions or specific addresses. This was a feature that could not be offered by ADVO with the undifferentiated, unlabeled marriage mail packages.

Over the course of a year or so following the development of the newspaper and labeled mail program, the *Chronicle* won back all of the grocery advertisers and has held that advertising category to this day.

The success of this program resulted from gathering information on the competitor's product and developing a complete understanding of the sales and production process. This information led to the development of a program for the *Houston Chronicle* that grew to be one of its key revenue sources.

I now teach marketing strategy courses to undergraduate and MBA students at the University of Houston's C. T. Bauer College of Business. These classes are divided into teams and work with real clients to develop specific marketing strategies during the semester. The first half of the semester is devoted to gathering information on the market, the competition, the company, and the environment. With this information and specific objectives set by the client company, students spend the second half of the semester developing marketing strategies.

In every case, students are told to look for that one piece of information that can contribute to developing a marketing strategy that can have a significant positive impact on the client companies.

In the example of the *Houston Post*, it was the financial tracking and the knowledge of the newspaper-purchasing program that led to the *Chronicle's* successful strategy.

For the ADVO example, it was the knowledge of the packaging and delivery process that allowed the development of a strategy to which ADVO could not respond.

For a marketing strategist, it is important to have a good understanding of the industry on which the firm will focus its efforts and the market in which it will compete. After identifying the industry and market, the strategy will be influenced, in part, by the competition. Knowledge on all three will be essential ingredients in a successful strategy.

Over the years, I have been involved in many strategic marketing efforts and every successful project can be traced back to developing solid information on the customers, the market, and the competition.

CHAPTER 2

Legal and Technological Changes

This chapter focuses on environmental conditions over which an organization has little or no control but may be able to develop a strategy that can take advantage of the new paradigm. Legal and technological changes are two of the most prevalent environmental impacts that can affect strategic marketing efforts.

A situational analysis should consider changes that may occur over which the organization has no control. Advances in technology and changes in the legal environment can be significant.

For example, the Affordable Care Act has and will have a significant impact on the health care and insurance industries. These industries had some influence on how the law was designed but, at the end of the day, the health care and insurance industries have little control over the effect the new legislation will have on their organizations.

For organizations that are affected by new legislation or changes in the regulatory environment, it will be important to adjust marketing strategies to meet the new operating requirements.

Technological changes can have similar effects. Personal computers have changed the landscape for media companies, retailers, health care providers, educators, and many more.

When developing strategies, understanding market innovations and identifying possible market disruptions can be critical. Knowing whether your organization is in an industry that can or will be impacted by legal, regulatory, or disruptive innovations can be critical to developing a successful marketing strategy.

What Is the Next Disruptive Technology?

How can you determine whether your company is at risk of attack from a disruptive technology? How can you take advantage of the next wave of business opportunities?

Clearly, if you can answer these questions you are well on your way to becoming the next billionaire. Since finding the answers will be challenging it is important to identify a process to review industries and businesses and discover indicators that might identify opportunities.

Clayton Christensen's theories on disruptive innovations can provide some insights. His theories show that disruptive innovations often are created when an industry leader's product has been improved to the point that a significant share of the market's customers do not want or need all of the product's attributes. This allows a new market entrant to provide a lower cost good enough product that does not have all of the bells and whistles of the industry leader's product.

This new entrant will attract the least profitable customer of the industry leader and be somewhat protected since it will be difficult for the industry leader to create strategies focused on its most profitable customer (wants all the bells and whistles) and its least profitable customers at the same time.

The new market entrant, as a result, is allowed to grow its customer base by attracting more customers who are satisfied with a good enough product. Over time, the new entrant improves its offerings and attracts more customers from the market leader.

To use this principle to spot emerging opportunities requires a bit of research and the ability to identify potential market disruptions. The recommended steps are as follows:

1. **Identify markets ripe for disruption:** A market ripe for disruption is one where the profits are very high and the mid-to-lower profit range customer base growth is at a point where it is stagnating or possibly shrinking. This is an indication that the products provided might have reached the point where customers may not want or need all of the attributes offered or that the price is reaching an unacceptable or unsustainable level. An example might be the health care

industry. Here the cost of medical care has reached the point where health care without insurance is difficult to afford. Further the costs are driving up insurance costs to the point where insurance is difficult to afford. While the total market for health care remains large and the demand is high, the lower profit segment is stagnating and some are foregoing all but critical health care. The Affordable Health Care Act may bring insurance costs down and make health care available to a larger segment of the population. This will likely spur technological solutions for health care and provide market opportunities for good enough products that are effective such as a mobile phone application that allows a clinical assistant to provide a diagnosis and treatment for certain noncritical maladies.

2. **Identify new market entrants that are focused on the industry's least profitable customers:** New entrants would be providing products that are less expensive than those provided by the industry leaders. For health care, it might be the clinics operated by nurses that are located in grocery stores and drug stores. Another entrant for health care might be the telemedicine technologies that can provide diagnosis and some treatment protocols via telecommunications. For retailers, a disruptive technology was rural free delivery (RFD) mail service that spawned the catalog business in the late 1800s.

3. **Make sure that the new entrants are disruptors:** There are certain new technologies that might appear to be market disruptors, but are in fact sustaining technologies that can be used by market leaders to better serve their best customers. The Internet, for example, is considered a disruptive technology for the newspaper business. The problem with this conclusion is that the Internet market entrants targeted the newspapers' most profitable customers. This, in the short run, had a significant impact on newspapers but it also allowed newspapers the ability to focus on counter strategies. That is, the new entrant did not focus on the least profitable customers that would have created a dilemma for the newspapers to have to abandon very profitable customers to protect a marginally profitable customer base. The result is that newspapers and media companies have integrated the Internet into their businesses and are beginning to develop new digital strategies.

4. **Create an analysis that compares opportunities across industries:** There may be similarities across industries that provide very large opportunities. RFD mail delivery provided an opportunity for retailers to reach new communities by providing noncustom, good enough wares to be ordered through the mail. This delivery also allowed opportunities to printing, graphic, and media industries. The Internet has been a boon for social networking, search engine, and retailing but quickly became a key component for the delivery of new technologies such as telemedicine and energy production digital technologies.

After going through this process there will be a large number of choices and even the best analysis may result in a less than optimal choice. The analysis will, however, likely increase the probability of identifying a potential market disruptor.

Possibilities for the next big disruptive technologies include the following:

1. Telemedicine: This will provide the ability to deliver quality health care globally with smaller facilities onsite. The new technologies will include biomonitoring and feedback, microrobotics, and high-resolution, 3D teleconferencing during diagnosis and treatment.
2. Energy: Hydraulic fracking will continue to provide energy at lower costs. This technology will allow expanded global manufacturing capabilities in the United States as well as developing nations.
3. Education: Internet-based college courses and degrees will increase and allow more training that directly impacts career development. College degree costs will drop and access to top tier universities will be available globally.

When developing the *Houston Chronicle's* delivery program to compete with ADVO it was a careful study of how the labor unions influenced postal carrier routes. Some routes were pieced together with segments that were not necessarily contiguous. This meant the only way that ADVO could compete for address specific delivery would be by changing their entire model. We, on the other hand, started with address specific requirements and were able to build a model that married newspaper and mail delivery in a way that could not be challenged by the competition.

Conclusion

For a marketing strategist, understanding technological and legal barriers may allow the development of programs to capitalize on the barriers in a way that creates a stronger market position.

CHAPTER 3

Defining the Target Market Approach

A situation analysis requires, as pointed out in Chapter 1, a clear definition of the market to be served and an understanding of how that market can be approached to benefit the organization.

In their book, *Blue Ocean Strategy*, W. Chan Kim and Renee Mauborgne developed the Blue Ocean Strategy Canvas. This canvas allows the ability to look at customers and an industry over several dimensions in order to identify new market opportunities where the competition is irrelevant. The diagram in Figure 3.1 shows how a Blue Ocean Strategy Canvas was used in analyzing the market and trends for Cirque du Soleil.

As with market size, market share requires a strategist to consider individuals who may use the offered products or services infrequently or never. For Cirque du Soleil, the market consisted of individuals who went to circuses but also suggested that individuals who attended themed programs

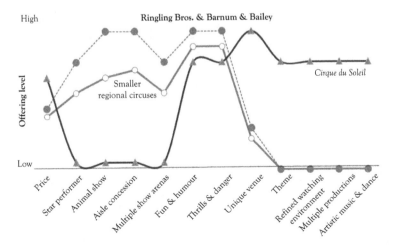

Figure 3.1 Blue Ocean Strategy for Cirque du Soleil

Source: Reproduced with permission: Harvard Business Press.

and unique venues might also make up the potential customer base. If the strategist combines the circus market with other entertainment venue markets the potential overall market is greater and the opportunity to create a larger market share is significant. Additionally, the strategy that draws from multiple venues will be difficult to be replicated by organizations competing for smaller market segments.

If I were to give a summary of the book it would be by using a quote by Wee Willie Keeler, a great baseball hitter in the late 1800s and early 1900s, who said, when asked the secret of his hitting success, "I hit 'em where they ain't."

At 5 ft 4 in and 140 lbs, Willie was a batting champion and is in the Baseball Hall of Fame.

For businesses, the *Blue Ocean Strategy* is a study on building a strategy for any business to "hit 'em where the competitors ain't." "Blue Oceans" are areas where there is little competition from rivals. "Red Oceans" are where rivals are congregated, fighting for customers using similar business approaches.

A place to begin a Blue Ocean strategy project is with the Strategy Canvas. This canvas depicts how players in an industry set their strategies on multiple strategy dimensions. You can see from the example in Figure 3.2 how Southwest Airlines strategy differs from the other airlines.

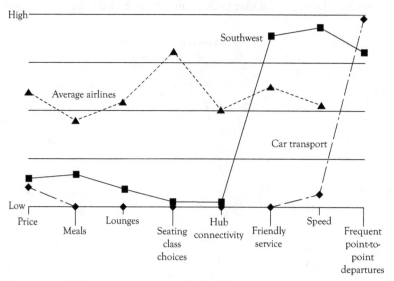

Figure 3.2 The strategy canvas of Southwest Airlines

Source: Reproduced with permission: Harvard Business Press.

This difference has led to Southwest's success in an industry full of failures and troubled airlines.

This is an excellent starting point for any company wishing to determine where to move strategically within an industry to find blue ocean waters.

Asking the Right Questions

Part of a situation analysis to define the market is developing an understanding of the environment that is free of bias. This requires testing assumptions and information that is gathered.

Often there is such a focus on running a business, closing a deal, or reaching an objective that attention is given to immediate outcomes. The result of this sort of intense focus is that it may cause a manager to miss important cues that affect the bigger picture.

I have been in countless sales calls where the potential client gave what could be considered buying signals and asked for more information to help in the decision-making process. I have seen good sales people put a very high probability that the sale would close based on this kind of customer feedback.

This can result in overly optimistic sales projections, which can have all sorts of negative consequences for an organization, including overestimating market share based on inflated sales projections. If a market is defined by faulty assumptions, the outcome will probably not meet expectations.

For example, one business associate said that he was approached by one of the world's largest manufacturers of a new electrical product to be their distributor in the United States. This indeed seemed like a real opportunity.

The associate was very successful and had a good reputation but was not in the electrical products business. I began to wonder why such a large manufacturer would approach someone not experienced in electrical products to open such an important market. Since my friend had asked me to join with him in this venture, I asked, "Why would the manufacturer choose us when they have access to virtually anyone in the world?" His response was that it really was not the manufacturer that wanted us as partners but a broker representing the manufacturer wanting to open a new market. Clearly still an opportunity but not anywhere near the scale that I thought was initially being offered. Here the potential market size and share is significantly diminished from the initial interpretation.

We have all been in situations like those described here and you begin to wonder if there is a way to get to the real meaning of a communication. I believe there is. It really focuses on stepping back and looking at the bigger picture and asking questions that might be appropriate. In the case of the electrical product manufacturer, it was appropriate to look at the bigger picture and wonder why such a large manufacturer would choose an inexperienced group to represent their products.

Questions can also turn a seemingly negative situation into one with a positive outcome. In one instance, a retail customer canceled an advertising contract with my company. The contract was for producing a weekly sales brochure. I asked why he would want to cancel the contract and the customer said "It doesn't fit our image." I asked, "What about the product doesn't fit your image?" and he said, " Well we are an upscale retailer." It occurred to me that the brochure was printed on quality paper but was primarily in black and white. I asked, "If we were able to provide a similar product in full color would it fit your image?" He responded, " We would buy immediately." Thus we went from a lost contract to a larger contract in the course of a few questions.

In this case, the answer to this question created a new business approach that allowed the organization to focus on customers who had not been targeted and as a result the organization's market share increased dramatically.

I am currently working on a proposal for a very large project that will engage our consulting firm for several years. The proposal is for a Central American government wishing to build new infrastructure components. We have met with the highest-level government officials as well as those responsible for managing the infrastructure projects. Everyone has assured us that we have the best expertise of any suitors and that we are preferred. In the meetings, we were asked to submit a proposal in the shortest possible time so that the government can begin moving forward with the proposed projects.

After the visits to Central America, we returned home and began thinking about the project. In the meantime, one of our team members had a conversation with an individual in the government there who suggested we submit two proposals. One proposal would be for an individual project and one for guidance to be provided for all infrastructure upgrades.

This all sounds very positive at this point but also brings some questions to the forefront such as "What should be different in the two proposals since we will be offering the same type of guidance in both instances?" or "Why two proposals?"

The answers to these questions will either limit or expand our opportunities in this country.

Asking the right question may seem like a trivial exercise but let me end with perhaps the most powerful example. I was visiting with a friend who is an oncologist at a prestigious cancer institute. She is most concerned with eliminating cervical cancer. This is an easily identifiable cancer and can be prevented by simply having a Human papillomavirus (HPV) vaccine administered to children from 9 to 12 years of age.

The HPV virus causes cervical cancer and Hepatitis B. Hepatitis B affects the entire population thus suggesting that the vaccine should be administered to males and females. Since the HPV virus is sexually transmitted, the vaccine must be administered when the immune system is naïve or unexposed to the virus. Thus the vaccine must be administered before individuals become sexually active.

This vaccine is well publicized and in the United States is highly controversial because of connotations associated with the HPV being a sexually transmitted disease. As a result, use of the HPV vaccine has found vehement opposition from religious and political groups based on the sexual nature of the disease.

My friend calls the HPV vaccine problem the biggest marketing blunder of all time. She maintains that if it had been introduced as a cancer prevention drug only, it would have been adopted and a lot of lives could have been saved. She wonders why the drug companies did not ask the question, "What is the biggest negative reaction to the introduction of this vaccine likely to be?"

For a marketing strategist, the question might have been "Is the market cancer patients or individuals wanting protection from the HPV virus?" In this case, the answer may not be about market size but market importance.

My friend tells me that in today's society introduction to the HPV virus is inevitable and that if you want to prevent the disease get the vaccine. Mentioning sex or sexually transmitted diseases is only counterproductive and opposition to the vaccine might have been avoided if someone asked the right question.

Conclusion

Understanding the market and the competition can provide advantages that make the competition irrelevant due to the creation of blue oceans. Further analyses and understanding of the market can prevent entering into a business too quickly or presenting the product in a way that will limit its success.

CHAPTER 4

Customer Jobs to Be Done

Developing a situation analysis requires that needs that exist in the marketplace be identified. How do you identify market needs? How do people come up with ideas that people don't know they need until they see them?

As we have discussed, a simple step-by-step process to create a marketing strategy begins with the identification of market needs. After deciding on the objective, it is necessary to create the guiding principles of the organization. This is best demonstrated by the following exercise. For this exercise, assume that you have decided that you would like to open a bar or pub.

1. **Create a vision and mission statement for the business:**
   Your mission statement might be:

   - To provide a place (in a geographic area) that will provide a friendly atmosphere for people to gather for social and business functions
   - To provide a selection of fine alcoholic beverages and hors d'oeuvres
   - To provide a venue that will attract key business, political, and community leaders

   Your vision might be:
   To create a place that will attract celebrities and community leaders by:

   - Attracting high caliber wait staff and mangers focused on customer satisfaction
   - Creating a facility design that allows patrons to hold private discussions

- Establishing the facility in an easy access high security area of the community
- Working with vendors to provide new and old favorite selections on the drink and hors d'oeuvres menus
- Maximizing long-term financial returns for shareholders
- Working with media outlets as partners to promote the exclusive nature of the business

2. **Identify the job to be done for the consumer:**
You can begin by thinking why people come to a bar and what they might expect. These are the jobs the bar is being "hired" to do.

As a partial list we might find some of the jobs are

- Social interaction;
- A source of food and drink;
- A place for entertainment;
- A business meeting place;
- A place to meet friends;
- A source of status (e.g., a place where important people gather).

3. **Look at the marketplace:**
It will be important to learn as much as possible about bars in the market.

Things you'll need to know are how much money is spent in the market at bars, restaurants, and similar types of businesses.

Information is available from sales tax data as well as industry sales sources that can be helpful in determining the size of the market, the average revenue per establishment, the average amount spent by consumers, and so on.

This information will be very useful in determining the competition and the strategy that should be employed. For example, it may be desirable to look at high-end bars and restaurants if they generate the highest revenue. This doesn't necessarily equate to profit, and deeper research may show that smaller bars have more consistent revenues and a higher profit percentage (not absolute dollars) than the high-end bars.

Obviously, the strategies for a neighborhood bar and a high-end club will be different, so it will be important to decide what you have as a driving motivation or vision.

4. **Using the vision and mission statement, create a strategic plan:**
The overall strategy for the business outlines how you intend to create the organization envisioned in the vision and mission statements. The strategy might be: To attract a patronage that will simultaneously benefit from being seen at the bar while providing status to the bar as a VIP gathering place which will, in turn, allow pricing and marketing to reflect a premium market position. This will be accomplished by

- holding events that will attract high profile individuals;
- holding events that will attract leading media coverage;
- inviting key community leaders to conduct business luncheons in the bar's meeting rooms;
- offering to sponsor charity entertainment events;
- using premium pricing strategies;
- hiring and training quality wait staff;
- offering high-end beverages and hors d'oeuvres.

Starting with an understanding of the jobs an organization is being hired by customers to perform can provide clarity for the marketing strategy development process.

Boston Globe and Washington Post

The newspaper industry may be the poster child for not being able to identify the job for which their businesses were hired to do.

It is interesting news that the *Boston Globe* sold for $70 million and the *Washington Post* sold for $250 million. These newspapers would have commanded at least five times that selling price a decade ago.

This is further evidence that print media is in trouble. The question is whether the trouble is truly from the presence of digital products or from management's inability to change the business model of newspapers due to the changing needs of consumers of information. It seems that there is tremendous demand for information but what is the job a news organization is being hired to do? Perhaps it is not only about the delivery of news and information but the ease with which the news is obtained.

In this regard, it appears that the Amazon.com approach to building customer relationships has a better chance of success than most. It also appears that the owner of the Boston Red Sox, John Henry, has a better idea of how to engage an audience than most.

I have spent a lot of time studying the effect of the digital age on the newspaper business. The digital age offers a lot of advantages with respect to the immediacy of news and the facilitation of the marketplace. There is no news happening on the planet that isn't available to the general public on an almost immediate basis.

Still, the printed newspaper has a following. The *Wall Street Journal* recently listed the top 10 newspapers by circulation:

1. *The Wall Street Journal*: 2,378,827 (includes 898,102 digital editions)
2. *The New York Times*: 1,865,318 (includes 1,133,923 digital editions)
3. *USA Today*: 1,674,306 (includes 249,900 digital editions)
4. *Los Angeles Times*: 653,868 (includes 177,720 digital editions and 43,275 branded editions)
5. *Daily News of New York*: 516,165 (includes 155,706 digital editions)
6. *New York Post*: 500,521 (includes 200,571 digital editions)
7. *The Washington Post*: 474,767 (includes 42,313 digital editions and 1,305 branded editions)
8. *Chicago Sun-Times*: 470,548 (includes 77,660 digital editions and 208,087 branded editions)
9. *The Denver Post*: 416,676 (includes 192,805 digital editions and 10,041 branded editions)
10. *Chicago Tribune*: 414,930 (includes 46,785 digital editions)

These statistics show that there is still demand for a printed newspaper product and a growing demand for digital newspapers. Part of this demand is based on the "comfortableness" factor of an audience that likes the regularity, familiarity, and credibility of newspaper reporting.

An area to really study is the growth of digital newspaper products. These products are usually a digital copy of the printed product. They carry all of the printed product's attributes to a purely digital format. This is different from the newspaper's website which will not have the feel or look of the newspaper.

I have written in the past about the advantages of advertising frequency and constant reach of an identifiable audience that are lost when the focus is on a website as opposed to the printed or digital editions of the newspaper. While these are real losses they will probably not be the critical factors in saving newspapers.

The critical factors will be in understanding the audience and the jobs it needs done and building a bonding relationship with that audience. Here, Jeff Bezos and John Henry excel.

If you have ever done business on Amazon.com, you immediately realize what a friendly experience is provided. My wife recently tried to buy a water filter for our refrigerator from the manufacturer. She spent about 30 minutes on line and was completely frustrated. She then thought she would give Amazon.com a try and about 3 minutes later she had ordered and paid for the filter. There are a lot of commerce websites but Amazon .com stands at the head of the class for creating an experience that invites customers to return.

While in a different business, John Henry has consistently had one of the highest attendance records in major league baseball. I was visiting with a friend who managed the business side of the San Francisco Giants who said that it was important to understand baseball is competing with all forms of entertainment. The critical factor was making certain that the crowd enjoyed the total experience. This is a lesson that is not lost on John Henry.

News will continue to be important and building a consistent audience will be critical to creating an advertising base to make a newspaper a profitable enterprise. Taking elements of the old model and melding them with elements of the new while creating a bonding relationship with the audience will be critical. I think these two entrepreneurs have the ability to apply insights from their past successes to their purchases of newspaper organizations.

Understanding that today's consumers of news are looking for news and information on their terms of relevance and ease of acquisition will be key in the development of news media.

Affordable, Quality Health Care Through Disruptive Innovations

Understanding the jobs that customers are asking to be performed will have an impact on how health care evolves in the United States. For the most part, the health care consumer wants access to affordable health care.

It doesn't appear that government intervention will solve the issue of providing affordable health care. Indeed, Medicare coverage is likely to diminish at a time health care cost is increasing. Further, it appears the efforts to cover the uninsured will only increase the overall health care costs. It doesn't appear that advances in technology and medicine are providing health care that is more affordable.

The medical community continues to march forward in its ability to cure the most deadly diseases and rebuild the most broken human bodies. For individuals to benefit from the advances in drugs, surgical techniques, and other medical advances, it requires a good deal of money or the very best insurance (also a good deal of money).

There is a chance that new entrants in the health care market space will find ways to reduce costs and provide quality health care. These entrants will likely be disruptive innovators and enter the market by serving the least profitable health care consumers.

According to the theories on disruptive innovations, new market entrants known as disruptors, find ways to profitably serve markets where industry leaders can't make a profit.

In the health care industry, profit is least likely to be made when the customers are uninsured and poor. The most profitable customers are those who have insurance, can afford insurance deductibles, and the ability to cover costs when they are not covered by insurance.

If a disruptor were to enter the health care market and focus on the least profitable medical customer, the industry leaders would likely not compete for that group of customers. Even if the industry wanted to find a way to serve the least profitable customers, they would find it difficult to change from the business model focused on delivering high profit margins. This has been validated in the past and discussed in length in Clayton Christensen's books and articles.

In the United States, we are seeing some health care disruptors such as clinics at retail outlets and drug stores. These are less expensive and not as time-consuming as visits to doctor's offices. This is a step in the right direction but not a disruptor that would address the high cost of hospitals, insurance, and specialized medical care.

Finding markets that will be large enough to stimulate real change are not likely to be in the United States or countries with highly developed economies. This is due to an unyielding medical infrastructure that is supported by both consumers and government. The move to quality, affordable health care in these countries will require changes in business structures that are profitable and benefit large segments of the population and changes in government support systems that are valued highly by large segments of the population. These changes will be met with great inertia.

Which Markets Will Stimulate the Disruptive Innovations for Health Care?

Developing nations that have limited medical facilities, a scarcity of top tier physicians, and limited government funds for health care will likely be the driving force to serve the planet's least profitable health care customers.

There are some countries in South and Central America that are attracting U.S. companies to provide expertise in building their health care industry. What the U.S. companies are discovering is that

1. the countries do not have the funds to build U.S. style facilities;
2. many of those countries' best doctors have moved to countries where they can earn more money;
3. the population is unfamiliar with preventive medical techniques;
4. the government's ability to support health care programs is limited by a weak or stagnant economy.

For the health care industry to profitably serve patients in these countries, it will require:

1. A larger population base being served by a smaller number of physicians. This will likely require smaller clinics located throughout the country that are manned by nurse practitioners and connected to larger hub hospitals by telemedicine technologies;
2. The development of telemedicine technologies that provide accurate analysis and treatment when used by minimally trained staff or private citizens;
3. Continued development of low-cost telemedicine that will allow physicians at hub hospitals to perform procedures at outlying clinics;
4. Programs to train personnel to serve in outlying clinics;

5. Regular educational programs focused on preventive medical procedures;
6. Insurance programs focusing on providing coverage for major medical procedures and providing incentives for participation in preventive medical programs.

While these approaches will make a big difference in undeveloped countries, they are unlikely to be adopted quickly by the developed economies of the world.

For a disruptive innovator to be successful in countries with developed economies, it will require many of the components previously outlined for developing countries with developing economies. In the developed countries, the focus will need to be on poorer communities. These are usually located in urban areas and consist of groups of economically disadvantaged individuals.

Successfully changing health care costs in developed nations can be accomplished by building programs for the poorer communities such as establishing clinics tied to hospitals and the introduction of telemedicine to serve those populations through community-based clinics without increasing medical personnel. The approaches outlined for developing nations might be a good start for developing a health care system in the developed countries that can profitably serve the poor and uninsured in some of their communities. The overall result will be the spread of affordable, quality health care for everyone.

In the end, understanding what will work in these less profitable communities will help in understanding the jobs that all patients are hiring health care firms to perform. Developing products and services for these communities allows the disruptors to sidestep the current complicated nature of the health care market and develop systems focused on patients.

Conclusion

For the marketing strategist, the jobs that need to be done can be identified through potential market disruptions. These potential disruptions can provide new opportunities for companies to differentiate their products and services and position themselves to capitalize on market changes driven by consumer needs.

CHAPTER 5

Customer Segmentation

Marketing strategy for any business should focus on the customer. The business is built on satisfying the needs of its customers, any adjustment in marketing approaches should consider the customer as the centerpiece of the strategy, and any action taken should consider the customer's view of valuing its products. Classifying customer segments can help identify strategies to grow market share.

One approach that can be useful is to classify customers based on the amount of their spending. Spending used as a metric can help an analyst understand which customers provide the biggest impact on the business. Customer categories can be described as follows:

1. Key customers who represent high volume users
2. Customers who have potential to provide greater sales (underpotential)
3. Customers who are not users (nonusers)

This simple classification may reveal some important information. For example, a company may find that the key customers are located in a specific geography, be of a certain size, have a certain business orientation, or have other characteristics that may be useful in developing marketing programs to attract new customers. This analysis may also reveal characteristics that define nonusers of the company's products. Understanding the size of the nonuser and underpotential user markets and their characteristics may also prove useful in developing marketing strategies.

The classification of customers may be enough to launch an ad campaign or promotional efforts but may not be enough to justify new product introductions or significant changes in marketing strategies.

After customers have been classified, a business can look at its various products and services and analyze them on the price versus cost to change relationship between the business and the customer. This approach measures the price charged for the product or service and compares that to the cost a customer would incur to change from the product they currently use to an alternative product offered. This may be financial cost incurred for changes in the customer's facilities or mode of operations or simply the difference in price of the products. Opportunity costs may also come into play if a customer has to forego opportunities to adopt a new product. This analysis assumes that price is the critical factor to cause a customer to change. If customer service, guarantees, maintenance, and other nonprice issues are important, then additional analyses will be required.

According to this type of analysis, when there is no cost to the customer to change then there is **equilibrium**. This result assumes that the customer could change to an alternative product and incur no costs associated with the change.

When the cost to the customer to change is greater than the price charged then there is a **positive equilibrium** relationship, which may provide the current product provider the ability to increase the price of the product and thereby increase the profitability without jeopardizing the relationship with the customer as long as a positive equilibrium state is maintained. Again this assumes that price is the critical factor. If other factors are important and the ability to deliver those factors to the customer difficult, then increasing the price to the customer could cause the customer to consider other vendors.

When the cost to the customer to change is less than the price charged then there is a **negative equilibrium** relationship, which could provide the customer a reason to find a substitute product or service. This means a customer could change products and save money. This scenario may also be an indication that the business has some special strength that is not price related. A close study of this group might be useful in setting strategies for the first two groups mentioned.

This exercise, when completed, provides a starting point for a marketing strategy because customers have been divided into smaller groups for further study (see Table 5.1). The smaller groups help analysts determine whether an action taken to affect one category of customer will have a negative impact on another customer group. For example, if a price strategy change is employed to attract more sales from underpotential

Table 5.1 Table of segmenting customer categories

	In Equilibrium	Positive Equilibrium	Negative Equilibrium
Key Customers			
Underpotential Customers			
Nonusers			

customers who have a positive equilibrium status, it could result in a negative impact on key customers in the equilibrium or negative equilibrium categories.

As an example, a newspaper company might have an advertiser who would be classified as underpotential with positive equilibrium (this is a customer who still spends most of his ad dollars with other ad media and there would be a real cost to this customer to move more advertising to the newspaper).

A strategy to offer this advertiser a lower price for increases in ad expenditures that would offset his cost to move advertising to the newspaper might seem to be in order. The downside of this move might be that there are key advertisers in the negative equilibrium or equilibrium categories (these advertisers could move away from the newspaper at no cost or actually save money) who would now face competition from the newly attracted underpotential advertiser. This situation might result in key customers diverting ad dollars to other media or require a price (and profit) reduction by the newspaper for key customers in the negative equilibrium or equilibrium categories.

Another example might be a consumer who purchased groceries at a new store offering very low special pricing. As soon as this pricing reverts to the higher, nonpromotional pricing, the consumer will return to the retailer in which a positive equilibrium relationship exists.

In both of these instances, it might be better to use a marketing strategy to attract these customers that is not based on price. Product attributes other than pricing may be instrumental in marketing strategies to attract these customers.

The customer categories can be combined with the equilibrium categories, so there are now three equilibrium categories for each of the customer classifications. For example, there would be key customers who are in equilibrium, key customers with positive equilibrium, and so on.

Customers in negative equilibrium may not be concerned with price as much as they are with intangibles such as customer service or long-term supplier relationships. Key customers in the negative equilibrium category are likely to be very profitable and can be subject to special attention by competitors.

Nonusers in negative equilibrium may be those customers who belong to the competition and who purchased when their regular supplier was unable to provide product. This group could be worthy of further study and could be an opportunity to win profitable market share from the competition.

From a company point of view, the area of greatest concern would seem to be those products with a negative equilibrium relationship for their customers. Negative equilibrium means that these customers could change products and save money; thus they are vulnerable to aggressive attack by competitors. Since this group is paying more for the product or service than they would from another source, it is very important to understand where they are placing the value of the business relationship.

It would also appear that those customers with a positive equilibrium relationship would be satisfied with the relationship with the organization because changing to another vendor would be more expensive than continuing the current business relationship. There may be an opportunity to increase pricing with this group but it is necessary to understand how much a price can be raised before moving the customer to a category that might be likely to find another vendor. It is also important to understand whether there are other factors affecting the relationship.

Those customers in equilibrium may be worthy of in-depth analysis to determine which factors could cause them to change suppliers since price is not an issue (Randazzo 2013, 63–66).

The approach outlined in this chapter is a useful way of segmenting customers. It allows a marketing strategist to understand the customer base from the standpoint of their willingness to consider alternative products. These groupings can then be further segmented by demographic and psychographic characteristics. When fully analyzed, these findings will be very useful in product design, pricing promotion, and product distribution strategy development.

CHAPTER 6

Challenges Faced

Internal and External

A situation analysis must include a critical view of the challenges faced by an organization. This is usually accomplished by conducting a strengths, weaknesses, opportunities, and threats (SWOT) analysis. In a SWOT analysis, the organization studies its strengths and weaknesses and the market's threats and opportunities.

Strengths and weaknesses are internal to the organization. Weaknesses can be strengthened and strengths can be exploited. Opportunities and threats arise outside the influence of the organization but can be addressed through strategic planning.

Strengths can include, the organization's image, relationship with customers and the community, employee quality, management stability, production efficiency, quality control, and so on. Each of these organizational characteristics can also be a weakness. An analysis of an organization's strengths and weaknesses must be unbiased to be effective.

Listing perceived strengths is a good starting point. Shown in Table 6.1 is an example of a list that might be developed for any company:

Table 6.1 List of strengths and weaknesses

Strengths	Weaknesses
Key management tenure	High employee turnover
Strong cash balance	Production equipment is old
Low number of days in receivables	Lack of new products
Outlets are near key customers	Outlets are not near growth areas
Good relationship with suppliers	High production waste
Strong operating margins	Poor production statistics system
Positive image in the community	Poor market research

Note: Each of these strengths or weaknesses can be addressed internally.

Table 6.2 List of threats and opportunities

Threats	Opportunities
Competition is introducing high-quality, low-cost alternative	New markets from developing nations' economies
Industry slowdown is likely next quarter	High availability of new college graduates
Government quality controls are likely	Some government credits are available for certain production improvements
Labor unions are wanting higher wages	Vendors are offering substantial discounts for key customer commitments

A similar table can be built for threats and opportunities. An example is shown in Table 6.2. Also note that the firm cannot change any of the threats or opportunities but can only plan or take advantage of their occurrences.

These are short lists. For a marketing-strategy situation analysis, this list would be lengthy enough to provide a clear assessment of the challenges to be addressed by the organization.

To create a complete list, it is a good idea to create a group of leaders from the various organizational functions. An engineering department may well be able to identify a weakness in the sales group and vice versa. The more complete the list of strengths, weaknesses, opportunities, and threats, the better the strategic planning will be.

After the list is created, it might be a good idea to review the list critically to see whether there are insights that can lead to additional items to be listed. For example, a strength that is shown here is the tenure of the key management staff. Listed as a weakness is high employee turnover. Further investigation might be needed to determine whether there is a relationship between long-term managers and the high turnover.

Also, high production waste and strong production margins might suggest that with better production quality control, prices might be lowered to compete with the competition's new product offerings.

After listing and vetting the lists of strengths, weaknesses, opportunities, and threats, actions should be listed that can address one or more of the SWOT items.

Some actions could address several items. For example, implementing a solid production statistics program could lead to programs to reduce

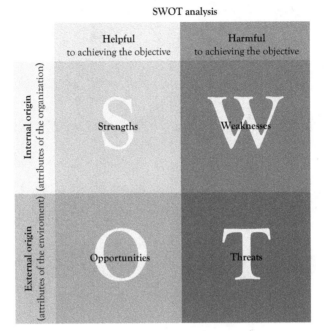

Figure 6.1 SWOT analysis

Source: Wikipedia Commons: Julio Reis.

production waste and reduce overall costs. This allows the ability to lower customer pricing while maintaining high operating margins. The previous matrix can be useful in developing a SWOT analysis (see Figure 6.1).

Next Steps

Having completed a situation analysis, an organization should understand the nature of the market, have a clear fix on the target market, understand the nature of the customer base, and have a set of actions to address the internal and external challenges.

At this point, the organization is ready to begin the development of a marketing strategy.

Figure 1. SEM/T nodule

Mean Slope

PART II

Vision and Mission Drive Strategy, Then Tactics

Having completed the situation analysis, you have identified the starting point of the strategic marketing trip. You know where you are with respect to the market, the condition of your vehicle, the resources available, and the condition of the environment in which your company will operate. The next step is to identify where you want to go as an organization and that as you lead the organization you have a guiding vision to keep you headed in the right direction.

This section of the book will focus on developing a vision and mission driven marketing strategy.

CHAPTER 7

The Vision Driven Strategy

The chart in Figure 7.1 and the following chapter demonstrate the approach for developing a successful marketing strategy. The graphic suggests that a vision (how the organization will create value for customers and stakeholders) and mission (the purpose of the business) should drive the price, place, product, and promotion marketing components and that once these four Ps are identified, a strategy can be developed.

To determine the value of each of the four Ps requires a vision and mission statement that clearly defines the nature of a business, the market segment to be served, and an idea of what success looks like. This vision and mission are the driving forces behind the development of the strategy. The strategy defines the parameters for the planning, organizing, directing, and controlling functions of a business. When the strategy is set, it defines the impact on the organization's workforce, cash requirements, operating procedures, and capital equipment requirements.

For my classes at the University of Houston's C. T. Bauer College of Business, I have used the example of an individual with a pressure washer and limited funds wishing to enter into the maintenance business and grow to be a major player in home and commercial maintenance. This example was also used in the introduction to this book.

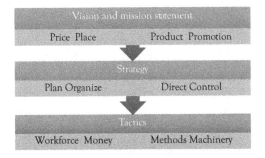

Figure 7.1 Marketing strategy flowchart

Source: Copyright GWR Research (2013). GWRResearch.Blogspot.com

This individual might create a mission statement as follows: (1) to make available quality exterior maintenance service to home and business clients throughout the state of Texas and (2) create value and make a difference.

The vision statement might be as follows: (1) using internal cash flows to develop an organization that provides exceptional quality service at reasonable rates, (2) create a network of technology and industrial partners to provide innovative and effective solutions for exterior building maintenance, (3) develop an organization that is highly effective, lean, and fast moving, and (4) maximize financial returns.

This vision and mission statement would help determine how the components of marketing would fit together to develop a marketing strategy. Since we know that it is to be a self-financed operation and that the only service now available is pressure washing, identifying the market that can be served now is important. The potential customers are those who need pressure washing but can't afford or don't want the services of well-established exterior maintenance companies.

After some consideration, a strategy statement might be developed. In this case, the marketing strategy statement might be: to market convenient, low-price pressure washing service to individual home and small business owners while adding services and markets as cash flow allows.

Here the P requiring attention will be promotion to efficiently let potential customers know of the service available. The place P will also be important in that the service should be offered only in areas that can be served with existing personnel and equipment.

It is with the vision and mission driven strategy that the planning, organizing, directing, and controlling components of management can be employed. At this point, strategy directs the development of the tactics that are in alignment with the vision and mission.

Planning would start with available resources and describe the process to grow from a single pressure washer driven organization to a statewide organization providing services to a large base of customers. The plan would describe the growth rate based on reasonable customer base growth and new services to be offered. The planning would consider the type of workforce to deliver the service (brokered, through other providers, independent contractors, employees, and so on).

The plan would describe the internal cash flows and the amount of cash to be used to maintain and grow the business. It would also describe approaches to increase cash flows, incur debt, or invite equity partners into the business.

The plan would also describe the types of equipment needed, when it would be needed, and whether it should be leased or purchased. Finally, the planning process would identify the methods by which the company would be managed from sales approaches to accounting procedures from quality control to credit management and job logistics.

After the plan is developed and compared with the vision, mission, and strategy, the business can set the organizational structure, understand how to direct activities, and create reports that allow management to gauge how closely actual results measure against planned goals.

This is a simple example but shows the importance of understanding what an organization wishes to do (vision, mission, and strategy) before developing tactics.

I recently visited with a young entrepreneur who had a small business that was seasonal. This entrepreneur also had a pretty clear idea of what he would like his business to grow to over time.

Faced with the need to fill in the off-season business cycles, he thought he would provide other types of seasonal businesses. While it was a reasonable approach, the seasonal business would not move his company toward the ultimate goal he had set for the business. I advised that using an approach of filling available work time with work that didn't support the long-term goals of the business could change the focus and perhaps prevent the attainment of the long-term goal.

Young entrepreneurs aren't the only people facing this dilemma. Seasoned chief executive officers (CEOs) find themselves faced with challenges and responding to market changes and competitors in ways that are not in keeping with the organizations' mission and vision. These CEOs are usually driven by short-term profit requirements and analyst's expectations.

It can be difficult to always go back to check to see whether the latest tactics being implemented to address a business challenge support the firm's mission and vision. It is also difficult to require that midlevel managers spread across many operating units only implement tactical solutions that are in keeping with the firm's overall mission and vision driven strategy.

But if implemented tactics are not in alignment with a mission and vision driven strategy, it is the surest way for an organization to find itself in an unintended business, producing value for unintended markets. This can spell financial ruin in the worst case, and in the best of cases, it will require a change in the mission and vision statement and direction of the business.

Strategy Before Tactics

An MBA student asked me not long ago whether I knew of companies that developed or updated strategies on a regular basis. He went on to say that he was in charge of providing information technology (IT) support for his organization and when asking for the strategic direction of the company he was told "to increase profit by X% in the next operating period."

This was clearly not a strategy but an operational goal. Operational goals are almost always addressed with tactical solutions.

The longer an organization has been in existence, the less likely a regular strategic planning process will exist.

Leadership will recognize changes in the environment, new financial goals, changes in operation procedures, new challenges, and competition. Almost always, tactical plans are developed to address the market changes and financial goals.

Tactical plans will include pricing structure changes, development of new products, new human resource programs, and new operational procedures. These plans can be very intricate and very sophisticated. For example, to increase revenues an organization might deploy a dynamic pricing program that provides different pricing for different consumers based on the perceived value to the customer at a specific time. This is a very sophisticated pricing program but doesn't qualify as a strategy. In fact, the tactic might be at odds with the intended strategy.

For example, if a company had a goal to market a product that would develop a deep loyalty with customers that was based on image, branding, and the ongoing relationship with its consumers, a dynamic pricing program might be viewed as opportunistic by some consumers and actually work against the overall strategy.

A good example of this is when Doug Ivester, former CEO of Coca Cola, mentioned that Coke might consider using vending machines that would charge a higher price as weather temperatures increased.

This move would not be in keeping with the mission:

1. To refresh the world
2. To inspire moments of optimism and happiness
3. To create value and make a difference

While this pricing move wasn't deployed, the fact that Ivester mentioned the possibility showed he was more of a tactical thinker rather than strategic. Here, Ivester forgot the importance of Coke to the consumers, which resulted in a huge negative reaction by the media and the market, even though the program was never implemented.

Coca Cola had another instance where tactics and strategy were confused. With the introduction of New Coke, Coca Cola forgot the history and the relationship with the market. By eliminating the original coke flavor and introducing New Coke, executives did not consider the value of the long-term relationship of customers with the original coke flavor.

The vision, outlined previously, should be the most important consideration in strategy development. Tactical considerations should then follow.

The over-riding consideration overlooked in both of these actions by Coca Cola was the relationship of the market with the brand that had been a part of the lives of individuals during the good and bad times of the twentieth century.

Interestingly both of these tactical moves might have been successfully implemented if tactical solutions had been designed to fit well with the overall strategy. For example, if vending machines had been deployed to give discounts when temperatures fluctuated, the company could have maximized margins and still provided the consumers with a positive view of the company. With the introduction of New Coke, keeping the original flavor would have provided a means of satisfying the psychological mystique associated with the founding brand while allowing consumers to try the new flavor.

Remembering to put strategy before tactics requires discipline to periodically review the company's mission statement and overall strategy and to make certain tactical moves are in alignment with the firm's strategy.

When determining whether a new program fits well with the overall strategy of the company, ask the following questions:

1. Profitability and market acceptability: Will the program generate a profit and a market?
2. Accreditation requirements: Does the program meet industry and legal standards?
3. Length of project: Can the program be introduced in an acceptable time frame?
4. Accommodate systems: Does the new program make use of current systems or will new ones need to be developed?
5. Fit image: Does the program fit the image the firm wishes to project?
6. Resources: Is the new program resource and capital intensive?
7. Gateway capacity: Does this program lead to the possibility of new products or businesses being developed?
8. Negative gateway capacity: Does this program have the potential of damaging other aspects of the operation?
9. Customer acceptance: Will the customer accept this program over others offered in the market (Randazzo 2013, 70–71)?

Plan for Possible Negative Outcomes

Unfortunately excellent strategic planning does not offset an entrepreneur's dogged desire to pursue a business idea regardless of the hurdles that must be overcome.

In one instance, I started a daily newspaper in a small town that already had a daily newspaper that was owned by a large communications corporation. The corporate daily had alienated the community and its advertisers, so I felt the timing was right for a competing newspaper. I attracted investors based on this premise and told them that only one newspaper would survive.

An end-to-beginning planning process was used and all of its elements were incorporated into a critical path or program evaluation review technique (PERT) planning process. The result was the creation of a newspaper from the ground up in 90 days. The staff was focused on serving the community and we were hitting the ball out of the park in market share and revenue gains.

I had pointed out to investors, only one newspaper would survive. It was apparent from the very beginning of the planning process that to be successful would require failure by the competition. We knew that it would be difficult but our dislike of the newspaper owned by the large corporation and our belief that we would win the community support led us to believe we could overcome any obstacle.

In *The Art of War*, Sun Tzu says that a force that is superior in size and resources will always win. To counter this strength, the smaller in the battle must capture something that is critically important to the one with superior resources.

In this newspaper war, the competitor had the resource advantage but we believed that a locally owned newspaper would gain the community support needed for a newspaper to survive. We felt this community support was the critically important advantage required by the eventual winner.

While that might have been true to some extent, it overlooked the ability of the competitor to focus resources on winning that support. Also overlooked was the real critical need for our competitor to demonstrate to other communities that starting a second newspaper was not a good idea. The competitor knew that if a locally owned newspaper succeeded in this market other markets could be in jeopardy.

In this case, we did not identify a specific item that, once captured, couldn't be regained by the competition (this would relate to items 8 and 9 in the previous section). The result was a victory for our competitor. Our strategy was a good one, our planning was flawless, and our efforts were valiant but we could not match the resources that the competitor could focus on the winning the battle.

A couple of years later I was brought into a similar battle, which we did win. In this case, we carefully identified a critical revenue stream that needed to be won. We identified this early on and the result was in fact a smaller newspaper winning the advantage over the larger corporate owned newspaper. Even so the corporation did not give up the market; it offered to purchase the new locally owned newspaper at a price the owners could not refuse. So in the end Sun Tzu was correct; the force with the largest store of resources won.

I tell these stories to caution entrepreneurs that while vision, commitment, strategy, and planning are critical, it is important that all obstacles to success be identified and dealt with realistically.

I have had successes over clearly dominant competitors and those successes required an objective study of the actions required and the potential reaction by the competitor. In most cases, victory was based on choosing a strategy that couldn't be reacted to by the competitor (a disruptive technology) or by feigning a move that caused the competitor to make a critical error.

This is one of the reasons I am in favor of end-to-beginning planning. This process, if used well, points up all of the potential challenges that must be dealt with to create a successful business.

The thoughtful manager will identify areas that can result in failure and plan accordingly.

There are some who will tell you that what will make the difference in these situations are managers who are critical thinkers. Theoretically a critical thinker is someone who is presented with an argument and can determine whether it is true, sometimes true, partially true, or false. Other definitions can be more detailed but this is essentially the gist of critical thinking. This simple definition assumes that the thinker sets aside emotional issues and any form of bias.

This is where the real difficulty lies. To be successful in assessing potential challenges, a manager must be completely objective. Let us take a simple example. Suppose you have planned to increase revenues by 5 percent for the upcoming year. To achieve this you might

1. increase rates by 5 percent and maintain current sales volume levels;
2. increase volumes by 5 percent with no rate increase;
3. increase some mix of rate and volume;
4. add new products;
5. add new customers.

Let us say that the planning process has uncovered a potential challenge to the 5 percent revenue increase—a new competitor with similar products offering discounted rates in order to gain market share. You are now faced with determining which mix of actions will most likely work.

If your company is the market leader with a strong reputation and image, you may decide that the competitor's strategy of offering low rates will fail and you choose to increase rates by 5 percent with no other actions required. You make this decision because there is a history of companies using these strategies to gain market share in the past and they have all failed to have any impact on your ability to grow revenues.

It is not uncommon for managers to choose actions based on limited and biased information. In using this approach, a manager may rely on past experience and his or her belief that the outcomes in the past will hold true for the future. Indeed projections based on history will work until they don't work—then the outcome may have very negative consequences.

Some would say that a critical thinker would be able to assess the argument that customers would accept a 5 percent rate increase without reducing volume and determine whether this claim is true or not. Then the best option for achieving a 5 percent rate increase would be identified and this action would be taken. Problem solved.

Here is the problem; this argument can only be answered correctly if perfect information is available. In fact, anyone can determine the correct answer if perfect information is available. Unfortunately, when it comes to projecting the future or human behavior there is no source that can provide perfect information.

Managers are forced to use history, intuition, biases, and beliefs coupled with as much data as is available to make critical decisions. Over the years, different mathematical projection techniques and gaming theories have been developed to help managers better predict outcomes but they still do not provide perfect information.

So what is a manager to do?

The end-to-beginning process can help identify challenges or obstacles in reaching a planned goal. Successfully addressing challenges requires developing a list of possible outcomes for each challenge and identifying the worst outcome. Once identified, a contingency plan should be developed that allows the overall objective to the plan to be achieved even if the worst possible outcome materializes. In our example, if the rate increase results in a volume decrease, then a plan should be in place to expand the customer base that allows the overall 5 percent revenue increase. This is a contingency plan that is ready for implementation should the need present itself.

The problem with contingency plans is that they take time to implement and they may be overly optimistic with respect to providing needed results.

Rather than having a shelf full of contingency plans, it is probably better to develop plans based on a certain degree of failure in addressing identified challenges. In our example, it might mean implementing a 5 percent rate increase plus setting a volume increase of 3 percent and developing new products and customer segments for yet another 5 percent. In other words, plan for possible negative outcomes in order to plan for success.

Conclusion

A company's vision and mission should be the over-riding factor in strategy development. We have introduced a checklist to help planners determine whether actions planned are in keeping with the vision and mission. We then show examples of how tactics are driven by a strategy. We also recognize that the best planning may still have deficiencies since planning assumptions are based on an uncertain future. The uncertain future can be somewhat accounted for in the planning process by developing contingency plans or plans that launch programs to offset potential failures before they occur.

CHAPTER 8

Product

This chapter focuses on a process, to find and develop products, that is in keeping with an organization's vision and mission. Within that framework, the discussion focuses on product development programs that are based on consumers' needs, provide innovative solutions, and match drivers of the consumer product adoption process.

Generating New Product Ideas

The first step in generating good product ideas that will further develop the markets and expertise that defines the firm is to clearly articulate the job customers are hiring the firm to perform. This should be in line with the original mission and vision statement.

It is important not to be too restrictive in the focus of the definition. It is probably better for an owner of a baseball team to define his firm's job as sports entertainment as opposed to the more focused definition of professional baseball.

As most newspaper owners are aware, it is better for them to be in the business of providing information rather than strictly the newspaper business. This allows newspaper publishers to consider multiple platforms to deliver information.

Once the job the customer has hired the company to perform is defined, then it will be easier to identify new product ideas that are based on the firm's strengths.

There are several methods to develop new product ideas that are very useful such as brainstorming, market research, and product attribute modeling.

Brainstorming is widely used and involves getting key employees (and sometimes customers) together to find solutions to challenges facing the firm. The key to successful brainstorming is good note-taking, allowing all ideas to be presented without negative feedback, and encouraging all participants to contribute without letting a few dominate the exercise.

Market research can be the result of research surveys designed to uncover market opportunities. This research involves current customers, individuals with characteristics similar to current customers, or a random selection of individuals. Examining a firm's records and reviewing sales staff information on the market and the competition can also provide solid market research. Focus groups are an inexpensive way to define customer's needs and test new product ideas.

Product attribute modeling is a unique way of generating new product ideas by choosing a job the company is hired to perform and describing the absolute worst outcomes. After identifying the bad outcomes, participants go back through the exercise and determine what actions could be taken to eliminate the negative outcomes. For example, if a company made suitcases, an exercise might be to list all of the negative attributes for suitcases (such as not fitting in overhead bins in aircraft, wheels that wobbled, instability, and so on). The follow-up exercise would be to create a suitcase that addressed all of the negative attributes.

The best idea generation will likely come from a program that involves all of the idea generation techniques: first, market research, then brainstorming based on the research, and finally product attribute modeling.

Identifying the Best Ideas

The simple truth is that the need is there and the job the new product will perform is one that needs to be done and may be getting done but not very efficiently.

So is there an exercise that can identify jobs that need to be done more efficiently or begin being done?

Here is a process that works. Go through this example and see whether it helps you develop a new product or business.

1. **Pick an ordinary person who is going on a business trip.**
   Here is a list of things that will need to be done:

   - Prepare for meetings
   - Make reservations for hotels, cars, restaurants, air travel, and so on
   - Travel to and from destination
   - Pack clothing and so on for trip

2. **Now break down any one of these categories to activities. Choose "Pack clothing for trip":**

   - Get suitcase
   - Lay out clothes for each day or activity
   - Layout toiletries and personal items for each day
   - Fold clothes to fit suitcase
   - Pack suitcase with clothing and personal items
   - Unpack at destination
   - Keep soiled clothing separate from clean clothing
   - Repack for return trip
   - Unpack at home
   - Rehang fresh clothing
   - Launder soiled clothing

3. **Now pick an activity that might lead to an innovative product:**
   Let us pick "Fold clothes to fit suitcase."

   There are numerous devices that are designed to help keep clothes neat in a suitcase. Mostly they don't work. So let's say we'll create a device that will allow someone to fit clothes in a suitcase and keep them neat during travel.

4. **First we might describe the worst outcomes of people trying to fit clothes into a suitcase:**

   - Suitcase is flexible and therefore will not hold clothing's form
   - Clothing is not uniform and will not fit evenly into a suitcase
   - Clothing gets wrinkled and must be pressed
   - Device to keep clothes neat actually creates unwanted creases or wrinkles
   - If suitcase is damaged or gets wet there is high probability clothing will be affected

5. **Now create the new product by addressing the possible bad outcomes:**

   - We could create separate packaging to put clothing in before putting them in a suitcase.
   - We could develop packaging that fits together in uniform fashion like building blocks to keep clothes in place during travel: one type of container for shirts, one for slacks, and so on.

- This packaging could allow clothing to be fitted on forms to hold clothing's shape and prevent wrinkles.
- This packaging would be watertight and durable to protect clothing even if suitcase is damaged.
- This particular example was created in about 30 minutes. With a group it might take longer because there will be more innovative thinking and more solutions that are better.
- This process can be used for any activity and it can be used for businesses in any industry.
- After the idea generation process, there are likely to be a number of ideas that are attractive. The challenge is to find a way of objectively identifying those ideas that hold the most promise.

For this process, it is important to assemble a committee of key employees from each part of the business. The committee should have members from sales, information technology (IT), finance, accounting, production, research and development (R&D), and engineering. This structure allows any idea to have the insights from the various parts of the organization. The committee should be led by an individual who can keep the group generating customer focused ideas and prevent efforts to kill product ideas because they don't fit with current thinking.

When evaluating new product ideas, just as when a marketing strategy is being evaluated, there should be specific criteria identified that the new product must meet before moving to the next level of consideration. A list of evaluation criteria, similar to that used in the previous section, might look like the following:

1. Profitability and market acceptability: Will the product generate a profit and a market?
2. Accreditation requirements: Does the product meet industry and legal standards?
3. Length of project: Can the product be introduced in an acceptable time frame?
4. Accommodate systems: Does the new product make use of current systems or will new ones need to be developed?
5. Fit image: Does the product fit the image the firm wishes to project?

6. Resources: Is the new product resource and capital intensive?

7. Gateway capacity: Does this product lead to the possibility of new products or businesses being developed?

8. Negative gateway capacity: Does this product have the potential of damaging other aspects of the operation?

9. Customer acceptance: Will the customer accept this product over others offered in the market?

If product ideas successfully meet all of the criteria then product ideas can be chosen to move forward to a product planning process. Those chosen as having the highest priority should best meet all of the criteria with the least organizational expense.

Product Planning

Product planning requires that the participants of the committee review each product based on its impact on their area of operations. This review should include all phases of the organization from design to production, marketing, and billing. This review will bring to light areas of concern that will need to be addressed before final planning begins.

The final plans that this committee produces will include financial pro formas and projections, marketing plans and goals, operational plans, and identifying points or outcomes that would result in termination or re-evaluation of the project.

In the end, executive management will approve or disapprove the project but they will feel certain that the new products presented have had the benefit of a rigorous, objective process to create products that are most likely to have a positive outcome for the company.

At the *Corpus Christi Caller-Times*, we developed this process for reviewing our customers and the markets we served in order to create new products and revenue streams. This program was so successful I used it at every opportunity. In Houston, we created a new product committee and enjoyed all the successes and breakthroughs I had come to expect from cross-functional teams.

Over the years, I was able to attend new product seminars and meet with the leaders of companies that had sophisticated new product development processes. I met with new product managers from Ford, 3M,

Proctor and Gamble, and others. It was clear that teams were a critical element of new product development but so was a process. In every case, these leading new product developers had a series of steps that took new products from the idea stage to the market. Most companies used a stage-gate process, which reviewed the product at each stage of development. If the product met pre-established expectations then the product was allowed to move to the next stage of development.

We created a similar process at the *Houston Chronicle*, which was then adopted by the Hearst newspaper group. We found that we were able to have several ideas and projects under review simultaneously and move good ideas into good products at a very fast pace (see Figure 8.1).

Ideas were accepted from anyone. Employees and customers provided the most actionable ideas. The first step was to evaluate the project in a broad sense. Did it complement the other businesses we operated and customers we served? Could it produce a profit? We chose only projects serving our markets and that would produce at least a 30 percent operating margin.

The next step was to screen projects based on their ability to create new revenue streams. This would require that they would create a market demand, be easy for our sales force to present to new and established customers, and fit well with our product mix and our operating systems.

We also considered the product's *gateway capacity* or its ability to generate additional products. For example, one of the reasons we chose to develop a relationship with the Spanish language publication *La Voz* was its ability to provide access to the Hispanic market and ultimately produce an array of products for that market.

The La Voz project not only filled the goal of reaching the Hispanic market but also taught us how to work with niche print publishers. Over the next few years the *Chronicle* entered into printing and distribution relationships with several niche publishers.

Defining Potential Actions

Having the right offerings that best meet the market needs at a price that is acceptable to customers and provides profitable cash flows for the organization requires a well thought-out product assessment process.

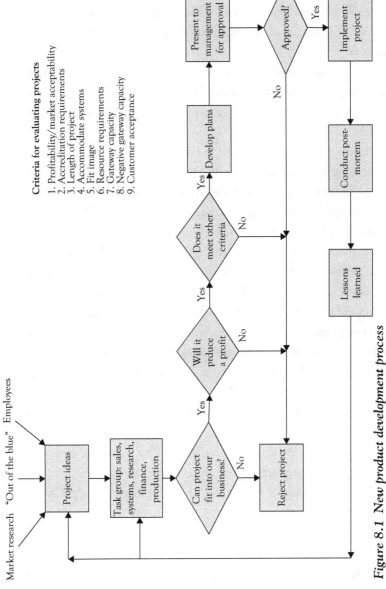

Criteria for evaluating projects

1. Profitability/market acceptability
2. Accreditation requirements
3. Length of project
4. Accommodate systems
5. Fit image
6. Resource requirements
7. Gateway capacity
8. Negative gateway capacity
9. Customer acceptance

Figure 8.1 New product development process

Source: Copyright GWR Research.
Reproduced with permission.

It is important to include a complete description of the product and the alternatives used in the comparison. The product description should include all tangible and intangible characteristics. Tangible characteristics would include size, weight, and other physical properties of the product. Intangible characteristics would include guarantees, customer service, and ease of understanding how to use the product or product training, and so on.

While tangible and intangible characteristics may be hard to capture it is an important exercise from the view of the customer. It helps understand the real job the customer has hired the company and its products to do.

Clayton Christensen gives the example of milk shakes being used in the morning as a breakfast substitute for people on their drive to work and in the afternoon as a reward mothers gave to their children after school. In his example, the milk shake had been hired to do two different jobs by two different customer groups. Clearly price alone could not describe the different jobs the product was hired to do nor could it describe the value of the product to either group. In the case of milk shakes, characteristics that would need to be included would be the availability of the product (this would fall under "search time intensity" in the following).

To help describe product characteristics, it may be useful to consider the potential actions to be taken in light of several "consumer adoption drivers" (CADs) that we developed at GWR Research.

1. Group influence intensity (GII): relates to peer pressure exerted on customers
2. Perish ability: the length of time the product is deemed useful
3. Psychological appeal: status associated with the product
4. Price sensitivity: the need for the customer to budget for the purchase
5. Relative price influence (RPI): the attractiveness of other products as a substitute when price is a consideration
6. Frequency of purchase (FOP): the frequency with which the customer purchases the product
7. Search time intensity (STI): the amount of time invested in the search for the "right" product

8. Tangible differentiability (TD): physical differences between products

9. Intangible differentiability (ID): nonphysical differences between products (guarantees, relationships with company, branding, and so on)

10. Technical complexity (TC): the need for training before a customer can use the product. This may be a factor in determining the type of sales force that will be required.

Table 8.1 arranges each dimension next to a semantic differential. Using a fairly simple research survey, customers can rank the dimensions as being of high, low, or no importance. Analysts can use questions that elicit responses for each CAD descriptor (Randazzo 2013, 67–70).

Customer Survey Process

Using focus groups to get a qualitative feel may provide a good start to identifying customer groups according to CAD.

For critical strategic decisions, customer groups should be large enough to provide results with a high level of statistical confidence. The key customer and underpotential customer categories may require a census to provide statistically significant findings. Nonuser categories are likely large enough to use random sampling techniques.

Table 8.1 Consumer adoption driver evaluation chart

Dimension	High	Low	None
Group influence intensity (GII)			
Perish ability			
Psychological appeal			
Price sensitivity			
Relative price influence (RPI)			
Frequency of purchase (FOP)			
Search time intensity (STI)			
Tangible differentiability (TD)			
Intangible differentiability (ID)			
Technical Complexity (TC)			

To make the analysis easier, the questionnaires would note to which of the nine categories (equilibrium key customers, positive equilibrium key customers, and so on) the customer belonged. This allows responses to be collected and analyzed by customer type.

Analysis of the Data

Using the example of luxury automobile consumers, an example of the CAD analysis is shown in the table that follows.

The following symbols are used to show how each equilibrium category, discussed in Chapter 5, responded:

Key customers—luxury automobile consumers

	GII	Perish ability	Psychological appeal	Price sensitivity	RPI	FOP	STI	TD	ID	TC
High	+		+ − =			+	− = +	+ − =	+ −	
Low	− − =	+ − =		+ −	+ −	− =				− + =
None	=			=	=				=	

Underpotential customers—luxury automobile consumers

	GII	Perish ability	Psychological appeal	Price sensitivity	RPI	FOP	STI	TD	ID	TC
High		+ − =	+ − =	+	+		+ =	+ − *	−	
Low	+ − =			=	=	− + =	−		= +	− + =
None				−	−					

+ represents positive equilibrium customers
− represents negative equilibrium customers
= represents customers in equilibrium

For the key customer categories of this company with positive equilibrium (they would need to spend more money than they are now to adopt the luxury automobile), GII was considered high. This means that the action of their peers would influence the type of luxury car they would purchase.

For those key customers who had negative equilibrium (they could change and save money) GII was low. Group influence intensity did not affect key customers who were in equilibrium. One could conclude then that certain key customers are influenced by their peers to purchase a particular luxury automobile while others were not. One could then assume that a marketing strategy that used individuals viewed as peers in ads would have a positive effect on the positive equilibrium consumers and no effect on the negative equilibrium or equilibrium consumers (a seemingly safe strategy).

For underpotential customers, it might be useful to target consumers in the negative equilibrium category since price is of little consideration to this group. What is important is ID. A marketing campaign focusing on the brand might be beneficial here and would not have a negative effect on any of the other key customer categories. Combining use of peer groups and brand in an ad might have the effect of reaching the key customer and underpotential customer categories effectively.

The process of using the CAD and cross-referencing the customer categories can be used as idea generators for strategic marketing initiatives. These initiatives can then be measured against a set of criteria, which helps analysts and managers focus on overall organizational goals.

Implementation of Chosen Actions

Success for this process depends on continual involvement by executives from each discipline in the organization's leadership. There should be a team formed of these executives that meets regularly (weekly) during the strategic review process.

The executive review team should have a representative from sales, finance, operations, marketing, human resources, and so on. Representation of the different business disciplines ensures that internal perspectives are considered for all potential actions.

An individual should be chosen from the group who will act as its leader and keep the team focused on producing results. Meetings should be held separately from other business meetings and functions to underscore the importance of the exercise.

The review process will likely take several weeks to several months to complete depending on the level of analysis desired at each step of the review process.

Concept Test to Validate New Product Strategies

How can you determine whether the latest new product idea will be a success?

As the potential organizational impact of a new product introduction increases, it becomes more important to find ways to improve the chances that the product will be a success.

The product creation process and the new product development process provide a structure to methodically develop and bring a product to market. These tools however do not determine the chances that the marketing strategy for the new product will be a success.

A concept test provides a simple inexpensive way to determine the appropriate marketing strategy and to project potential sales.

Here are the steps for implementing a concept test to validate the marketing strategy for a new product.

1. **Describe the new product:** The new product description should include all physical characteristics (this may include a mock-up of the product). Also describe marketing attributes such as price, where the product will be available and special promotional efforts.

2. **Identify targeted market segments:** Identify customer segments for which the product is intended; then, further subdivide the groups by demographic characteristics. For example, if the product were a new sports automobile the most likely customer segments would be current owners of sports cars. The customer segments might be people who only buy sports cars, people who own their first sports car, and people who do not own sports cars but have other characteristics in common with sports car owners. The next step would be to take these potential customers and categorize them by demographic characteristics. The resulting categories can be cross-matched with the demographic segments to provide a better understanding of the customer base. For example, one subgrouping might be females who

only buy sports cars, who are professionals, and are 25 to 35 years old.

3. **Develop a questionnaire to assess the product's physical and marketing attributes:** The questionnaire should identify key characteristics that will determine the product's appeal. In the case of a sports car, the questionnaire might be accompanied by a mock-up or artist's representations to make sure there are no misunderstandings when interviewing a respondent. Attributes that should be tested include: design, complexity, peer influence, pricing, intangibles (guarantees and so on), and availability (willingness to travel to purchase). Each characteristic should be measured along a scale that can be measured (for example, On a scale from 1 to 10, how would you rate the design?). Also include questions that measure the willingness to act (Of the following distances, which is the farthest you would travel to purchase this product? or Which of the following amounts do you think reflects the value of this product?).

4. **Conduct a survey of customers from various market segments including the targeted market segment:** The survey should include the broad customer segments of interest as well as those that are not considered to be likely customers. The size of the survey should provide a meaningful representation from each category. This approach will provide meaningful information about potential purchasers and people who may influence the purchaser but are not purchasers themselves.

5. **Compile survey results to determine market size and potential revenues:** After the survey has been completed and the results analyzed, there should be evidence that allows managers to develop an implementation strategy for the new product that has a good chance of succeeding. The analysis should show the demographic profiles of those most likely to purchase the product, how far they will travel, the price they will pay, and so on. The analysis can also identify some potentially harmful marketing tactics that might have been used if the concept test were not employed.

6. **Use weighted averages to determine the importance of product and marketing strategy components:** Using the scales to measure the value of each marketing component on the questionnaire,

develop averages for each subgroup and a weighted average for the total group. For example, let's assume people who buy only sports cars would travel 30 miles to buy the right sports car while first-time buyers would travel only 15 miles and the remaining general car buyers would only be willing to travel 10 miles. If the market were made up of 15 percent of the first group, 30 percent of the second group, and 55 percent of general automobile purchasers, then the weighted average of the travel distance would be $(0.15 \times 30$ miles$)$ $+ (0.3 \times 15$ miles$) + (0.55 \times 10$ Miles$) = 14.5$ miles, the weighted average distance the purchasing groups would travel. In this case, using the 30 mile distance people who only bought sports cars would be willing to travel as a guide for dealership placement would be a mistake. Moving dealerships within 14 miles of population centers would capture more sales.

We used this process for a new product group that had proposed several alternative products to address a market threat. All of the products seemed to address the market challenge and all of the products had been through the stage-gate approach used in the new product development process mentioned earlier.

The result of the concept test allowed us to: identify the most appropriate products for the market challenge; eliminate products that would have failed; identify the best promotion and pricing strategies; and estimate, with great accuracy, the revenues and profits the new products would generate.

Conclusion

This chapter has focused on developing products that are in keeping with the organization's vision and mission and satisfy requirements of consumers needing a job done. We have reviewed programs to generate new product ideas, develop new products, and identify CADs that can affect the new product's acceptance in the marketplace. Using these approaches helps a marketing strategist focus on projects that are more likely to match market and consumer expectations.

CHAPTER 9

Promotion

As with product development, promotion strategies must keep in mind the vision and mission of the organization. Within that context, it is necessary to understand the job that needs to be done and the impact promotion can have on the consumer adoption process.

A Process to Develop Effective Ad Media Strategy

The Dilemma

Today there are so many options for businesses to advertise their products or services to consumers that the decision-making process becomes difficult at best. The new technologies allow new methods of reaching potential customers and new marketing techniques provide different approaches to segmenting groups into meaningful audiences. It seems that each advertising medium has a logical story that suggests it is the best medium to use to reach current and potential customers. Here are some steps that will help design an effective ad campaign.

Determine the Job to Be Done

A business may want to reinforce relationships with current customers, attract new customers, introduce a new product, create a need for a product, or build an image. These are but a few of the jobs that may need to be accomplished and they each may require a different mode of advertising. The media that will work best will depend on the audience to be reached. It is likely that an advertiser will need to use several media. For example, a company wishing to strengthen its image as reliable with its current customer base and develop a new customer base with an image of being innovative might require one set of media for each set of customers.

For an ad agency, media executive, or chief marketing officer this is the most important step in building a successful ad campaign.

Once a clear understanding of the job to be done is completed, it is time to consider the type of media and the cost-effectiveness.

Determine Media Usage by Customer Segment

There is abundant information available on media use by demographic and psychographic characteristics. Matching each of the advertiser's customer groups using these characteristics with the appropriate media improves the chances that the targeted advertising message will reach the right audience.

It is important to note that a company's established customer base may have a different demographic profile than a new customer base that is targeted. For example, an Internet game developer may have an established audience that is young, single, and at the early stages of a career. This developer may also want to find a market in the business community for a program that allows business professionals to test various market scenarios. Reaching these two audiences will require considerable thought to message design and media choice.

Determine the Budget

It is important to understand the amount of money available to accomplish the task set for the advertising project. Companies usually know what they need accomplished and they know what their ad expenditures are to be kept within a certain budget.

The question becomes: How do you compare the cost of advertising between the various media? Here it is important to understand the cost of reaching an intended recipient. For media with subscriber bases and established viewing audiences, it will be easier to project a rate at which a target audience member is reached than for media that have not established viewership or that have models that tend to further fragment the market. For Internet programs with rotating advertising spots, it will be more difficult to determine how often the intended recipient is online at the same time the ad is being rotated into view. Similarly, search engine optimization (SEO) program success requires that the right keywords be matched with the intended audience. Here determining the right keywords and the likelihood that the intended audience will opt for search engine support is important.

It will be necessary to compare the cost of each medium to reach intended audiences. This will allow the development of a strategy that can use various media to meet an advertiser's objectives within the prescribed budget.

Where Possible Build Programs That Create Synergy Among Media Components

Recognizing that audiences are not pure in their media use will require the development of strategies that understand customer behavior and media cost. For example, an advertiser wishing to strengthen its image as reliable to current customers and present an image of innovation to attract new customers simply means that the message should translate to both audiences and be promoted using media that reach both audiences. This synergistic approach tends to improve media effectiveness while controlling ad campaign costs.

Moving an Audience to Act

Starting with the consumer adoption drivers (CADs) discussed in the previous chapter should provide some direction in developing communication to targeted customer segments. For instance, in the luxury automobile example, it appeared that group influence was important to key customers in positive equilibrium and of low importance to customers in negative equilibrium. It also appeared that both groups found that tangible differentiability was of high importance. One potential communication strategy then might be to create ads that focused on the physical attributes of the car. This would avoid any potential conflict from using individuals in the ads portraying roles of peers to the targeted audience.

Once the advertising approach is determined, the strategy of media and use comes into play.

Since advertising is the primary method for businesses to inform and influence individuals to consider and purchase their products, the question is often asked: How many advertising exposures are needed to cause an individual to act? Unfortunately there is no formula available to answer this question but there are considerations that can help.

Roger Wimmer points out that all people must pass through five stages to make a decision about anything or learn anything. These stages are (1) unawareness, (2) awareness, (3) comprehension, (4) conviction, and (5) action.

If bringing an audience from the stage of unawareness to the final stage of action is the goal, the frequency of exposure to an advertising message will be much higher than that which is required for just moving the audience from conviction to action.

Moving through all five stages probably would involve a product or concept that is new to the audience and the initial communication would have to educate the audience. The more complicated the product or concept, the greater the education requirements will be. For example, introducing a new drink to a market familiar with drink products will require less education than introducing insurance to an audience unfamiliar with the concept.

Moving from conviction to action is seemingly the easiest and should require the least number of messages to result in favorable action. This however is not necessarily the case. An individual may know there is a need for a product but may be hesitant to make a purchase due to budgetary restraints or the inability to make a choice from many similar products.

Identifying the Audience

Most businesses have a good idea of the composition of the target audience to receive advertising messages. The managers know the products, their uses, and the intended audiences. The audience demographic profiles can be fairly broad to very specific. For example, introducing a new computer would suggest those individuals who use a computer are the intended audience of the ad message for the computer. As it turns out, computer users come in every sex, age, or other demographic profiles. This can be further refined through CAD research.

Offering new roofing can be more specifically targeted to individuals who own homes 25 years old or older who have not purchased a new roof.

Classifying customers using techniques identified in the *Clarifying Marketing Strategy* of the previous chapter can be very helpful here.

Before designing an ad or message, it is recommended that some time be spent on understanding the audience by identifying the stage of the persuasion cycle, the demographic profile, and the specific message to deliver. In some cases, a general message delivered through a general reach medium provides an efficient, effective means of moving individuals to action. In other instances, a specifically directed message to an individual may be needed to result in action.

Understanding Media and Its Value to the Audience[1]

Choosing the right media for an advertising message should be considered as important as understanding the audience. Broad reach media should be considered effective when:

1. The audience is broad such as computer users or homeowners.
2. The product or concept is new and requires audience education.
3. The product is well-known and is available from many sources.
4. The product has different uses by different audiences.

More targeted media should be considered effective when:

1. The audience can be identified by three or more demographic characteristics.
2. The audience has a specific interest.
3. The audience has a specific ethnic, age, industry, or target profile.
4. Individuals or small clusters of individuals are targeted.

General circulation newspapers are an effective medium for broad market reach. In 2012, 42.9 percent of total adults in the United States read a newspaper daily and 44.0 percent read a newspaper on Sunday (Newspaper Association of America 2012). Advertising messages can be placed in various sections of the newspaper to reach certain subsets such as sports and

---

[1] Randazzo (2013), 81–84.

entertainment audiences. Newspapers also allow preprinted inserts that can be "zoned" to be distributed in specific zip codes or geographic areas.

Direct mail and shared mail programs provide the ability to reach the broader market or very targeted markets. The United States Postal Service (USPS) reports that 74 percent[2] of households read direct mail advertising weekly. Ad messages can be tailored to specific individuals or can be a uniform message to all recipients.

Radio and television have a broad reach but generally can't duplicate the reach demonstrated by newspapers or direct mail. Radio and television lend themselves to distributing messages to demographically unique groups that watch or listen to certain programming. While the viewing or listening audience may be large and diverse, radio and TV audiences usually will be smaller than those reached by a general circulation newspaper or a full market mailing.

Ethnic media provide the ability to reach meaningful audiences in a large diverse market. For example, in Houston, Texas, there are newspapers for the African American, Hispanic, Jewish, Chinese, Pakistani, and East Indian communities. Advertising in ethnic media may open access to markets that are not available through traditional media. These communities are large enough to represent significant purchasing power for products offered and the publications are usually reasonably priced.

The Internet has the ability to reach general and targeted audiences. An ad placed for general viewing on a high traffic site such as Google will be exposed to a wide array of web surfers. An ad that employs keyword searches can direct a very targeted audience to an ad or website.

Targeted or niche publications reach audiences that are smaller and have more defined characteristics but may still be quite general in nature. A Vietnamese newspaper in a large metropolitan area would still reach individuals who have a wide array of needs and interests. Trade magazines would reach more defined professional groups that comprise a large number of demographic profiles.

Outdoor advertising has the ability to reach the general audiences or targeted groups through the number and geographic placement of signage.

---

[2] Research study conducted for USPS by otal Quality Marking in late 2000

If an audience is reached by a medium, that doesn't mean the advertising message will be received. The ad may not be welcomed in certain media. The term *junk mail* was coined as a phrase describing advertising mail that cluttered the recipient's mailbox. TIVO and then cable ready versions allow television viewers to eliminate advertising messages. The popularity of these programs suggests that in certain instances advertising is not welcomed. On the Internet, the ability to screen junk e-mail and close or prevent pop up advertising also suggests that ad messages are not wanted at times.

What Is Effective Frequency?[3]

Effective frequency is the number of times a message needs to be delivered to the right audience to result in action and is within the cost constraints of the advertising budget. Effective frequency requires that the advertiser understand the audience, the stage of the persuasion process, the cost of delivering the message, and the best media to deliver the message.

For most products, the general audience medium is the best place to start unless the intended audience is a very small subset of the general population. General audience advertising can be supported with more targeted media to promote action. For example, adding ethnic publications may be a good way to reinforce advertising in the broader reach newspaper. These messages followed up with messages through Internet keyword searches or direct mailing will further enhance the ability to move audiences to action.

Another approach is to support a series of ads in a targeted medium with fewer ads in a general audience medium. Directing messages through keyword searches, direct mail, or targeted publications for specific audiences can be enhanced by an overarching ad in a general market media outlet.

The frequency of ads will generally be determined by an advertising budget. The mix of ad media should maximize the number of messages delivered to the targeted audience. If the budget is very limited and the target market is small, a well thought-out series of direct mail or e-mail messages may be appropriate. For example, a direct mailing to 10,000 chief executive officers (CEOs) might cost between $5,000 and $10,000.

---

[3] Randazzo (2013), 81–84.

If there were 10 messages needed to educate the CEO audience and lead them to action, a $100,000 budget would be required. An e-mail campaign could cost less.

If the desired audience were all CEOs in a large area, a general circulation newspaper would be a good choice. For around $10,000, a quarter page ad can be purchased in most major newspapers. If 10 messages were required, the newspaper budget would be $100,000. A positive consequence of this form of advertising is the reach of non-CEOs who would also have interest in the product. If the total number of CEOs in the market were 150,000, a direct mailing follow-up might be prohibitive and could be replaced with an e-mail or niche product advertising campaign.

Six Steps for Promoting an Idea or Business

Knowing your ad budget and developing an ad campaign is important but there are other actions that can be taken to promote a business.

If money is in short supply, it is even more important to develop a promotion infrastructure that can build your business. Here are some steps to create awareness if money is in short supply or to augment an ad campaign when cash is not a constraint:

1. **Create a "bumper sticker" statement or "elevator speech":** This is a simple phrase that explains what you do in a manner that sets you apart from the competition. This phrase is not only to make it easier to tell your customers what your business or product does, it provides a mantra for your employees, suppliers, and business associates to use. If done properly, it unifies the business and marketing strategies. IKEA, for example, in 1982 stated as its purpose, "To promote and support innovation in the field of architectural and interior design." Coca Cola's mission is to "refresh the world."

2. **Find ways to get publicity by tying to news articles and getting coverage:** Be on the lookout for opportunities to comment publicly or through press releases on topics that are germane to your business; for example, Whole Foods recent announcement that by 2018, all products in the United States and Canada must be labeled if they contain genetically modified organisms (GMOs). This was announced through a Whole Foods press release but was picked up by most mainstream media outlets. Here Whole Foods got in front

of the pack by making the announcement but giving plenty of time for implementation.

3. **Find ways of getting publicity by tying your business or idea to good works:** If there are charitable causes or organizations that fit well with your business model, a strong tie in can provide a boost. AT&T for example has established an office for a Chief Medical Information Officer that will focus on the use of telecommunications in providing health care. Additionally, AT&T has made numerous charitable contributions to organizations developing telemedicine technologies and procedures. While this is good work by AT&T for the community, it also positions them as a key player in the minds of telemedicine innovators.

4. **Start a blog that provides information that is relevant to your business:** A blog that is serious and provides useful information can build credibility for your business. American Express' blog on travel, http://www.travelandleisure.com/ provides very useful travel information that is tied to using the American Express card. Home Depot has a blog that provides information on home and garden projects.

5. **Use social network to link to your blog and update your networks on recent projects:** Facebook, LinkedIn, and other social networks provide a ready-made avenue to build an audience for your blog and to announce recent developments that may be of interest. Business Expert Press encourages authors to join social networks and to regularly participate in discussions. Since it is a step in the brand building process, this approach should be taken seriously. Comments on the networks should be in line with the image that you want to project to the general public.

6. **Form networks with professionals who augment or support your business:** Meeting with a group of similarly minded professionals can be intellectually stimulating as well as providing connections that can result in business. MFR Consulting recently created a group of senior advisors who have their own business consulting practices. These senior advisors meet monthly to discuss projects and ways in which they can grow the consulting practice. I regularly have a get together of friends to smoke cigars and drink some fine wine. From this group, I have been asked to participate as a consultant in two significant business ventures.

While a number of the aforementioned examples involve large organizations, the principles and approaches hold for businesses of any size. These six steps are fairly straightforward but they will require a commitment of time and focus to be successful.

Understanding What the Message Should Be

If you have developed a superior product that meets the customers' needs and made it easy to adopt, you may still find that your marketing message can be the problem.

I helped found a new commercial real estate sales company, American Property Data, in Houston, Texas. The concept was unique in that our company would attract listings from commercial brokers all over the country and present those listings to qualified investment groups located all over the country.

Success depended on attracting a leading commercial real estate broker in each market willing to sign on as an affiliate and feed their listings into the system.

Success also depended on qualified investors subscribing to our services and ultimately purchasing properties through our system.

Getting investors to subscribe to the service was relatively simple. If you were a qualified investor, a small subscription fee would certainly be a worthwhile investment.

Brokers, on the other hand, had to agree to a significant fee to be the exclusive affiliate in a market and had to be willing to share commissions on any property sold through the system.

There was no question that American Property Data was built around the needs of a commercial broker by providing a means of exposing his or her properties to groups of qualified buyers. This would not only allow the broker to increase sales but also to attract more listings and attract the best commercial real estate agents to come work with the broker.

Additionally the broker would not have to change how they operated their business. They would simply have a new tool that promised more sales opportunities.

The marketing communication difficulty encountered in the beginning was centered on our infatuation with the system's sophistication.

In the beginning, we talked about how the database was able to identify needs according to buyers' specifications and how we were able to have computers in buyers' and brokers' offices updated daily with new property information.

Unfortunately it was not the sophistication of the system that brokers were interested in. That information could come later. Eventually we learned the marketing message had to be on point and describe the benefits in terms that most mattered to brokers—getting more and better listings and attracting the best real estate agents.

This lesson was not lost when it came to me to introduce the *Houston Chronicle's* delivery system. Our program was presented by *Chronicle* senior staff members to advertising-buying decision makers. The message was simple—the *Chronicle* can reach all of the households currently being reached for a lower cost and better results.

It would be later that we would talk about the sophistication of databases and the ability to customize delivery. Interestingly, it was the customized delivery that allowed us to expand advertising delivery and commercial printing and produce new streams of profitable revenue.

Conclusion

Vision and mission driven promotion strategy has been the focus of this chapter. Much like the product strategy, it requires an understanding of the job to be done. This along with an analysis of consumer adoption drivers will help a marketing strategist determine the best mix of media and the types of messages needed to guide consumers in different market segments through the product adoption process.

CHAPTER 10

Pricing

The impact of pricing strategies can be critical for the success of new product launches, a company's image, and ultimately a company's short- and long-term success. The pricing strategy will affect the promotion, product, and distribution strategies, and must be in keeping with the organization's vision and mission.

Ten Considerations for Pricing a Product or Service

When introducing a new product or service to the market a key, and often critical, consideration is the price for this offering. I have seen folks simply take the cost of production and use a percentage markup as a pricing model. This is the simplest model and it provides a good example for the need to consider other pricing model options.

Here are 10 things to consider before setting a price for your product or service:

- **Markup based on cost versus retail:** In the opening paragraph, I gave the example of a model being used that marked up a product by a percentage over the cost. The cost used here is generally direct cost or labor and materials. If someone wants a 30 percent of the asking price to be marked up, then using 30 percent of the cost will not provide the desired outcome. Simply put, it is the wrong math. If something costs $1 to make and it is marked up by 30 percent for a selling price of $1.30, then the profit based on the asking price is 23.07 percent. To arrive at a 30 percent markup based on the selling price, it is necessary to divide the cost by its desired percentage of the selling price; in this case, $1 divided by its desired percentage of the selling price or 70 percent. Thus

$1/0.7 = \$1.43$. Here the markup is \$0.43 and is equal to
30 percent of the selling price. I know this seems simple but
I can tell you that it is a common mistake that is made by a
lot of business pricing strategists.

- **Competition:** It may not matter what you want to charge if
  your product has competition from similar offerings in the
  marketplace with similar capabilities. The price offered by the
  competition will have a significant influence on the price you
  will be able to charge unless you can find a way to differentiate your company or the product from the competition.
  Offering financing, volume pricing, or other supporting programs such as training or superior support services can accomplish this. If differentiation is not an option, then a review
  of the manufacturing and marketing processes may allow a
  reduction in the cost structure that, in turn, allows a greater
  profit per product sold even in a competitive environment.

- **Alternative options:** One of the major drawbacks of focusing
  on the cost of producing a product is the lack of focus on
  the alternatives that may be available to the customer. This
  can work for or against a pricing strategist. For example, in
  one company we developed a process for providing a service
  to deliver printed circulars in the newspaper and through
  the mail for considerably less than could be provided by any
  competitor offering the same service. One thought was to
  price the service with a small markup above our direct costs.
  This would certainly have drawn a lot of customers to our
  service but would have overlooked the possibility of pricing
  just below the competition or possibly above the competition
  and maximizing our profits. In the end we priced slightly
  below the competition, maximized our profits, and won the
  majority of the customers in the market.

- **Budget:** In every pricing situation, the customers' budget has
  to be a major consideration. If, for example, the typical customer spends 2 percent of their budget on products or services
  that you offer and your products require most or all of the
  2 percent, you will be forcing potential customers to evaluate

the potential expenditure very carefully. Many times to justify a large budget allocation, it will require more marking and support expenses on your part in order to clearly demonstrate the value of your offering. The question here is whether this approach will provide more profits or a larger market share (more profits) than competing with a lower price.

- **Knowledge:** In the early stages of a product life cycle, the consumer may not be aware of alternatives to your product or service and may allow the ability to charge a premium price. As you know, premium pricing and high profits will attract competition and competitors will work hard to educate consumers on alternatives to your offerings. To the extent you can hold on to the "knowledge differential" through patents or other protections such as capital requirements, you will be able to enjoy premium pricing. Be prepared to have a strategy when this advantage is lost. Some companies will schedule new product launches at the point where their patents expire.

- **Cost to produce:** As mentioned earlier, a clear understanding of the costs involved in producing and delivering your product or service plays an important role in pricing. Understanding the costs well enough to find alternatives to production or distribution costs can have a significant impact. Back in the days of phone modems, transferring data resulted in huge long distance telephone bills. One option I found was to work with Western Union and use their satellites to disseminate information around the country. This was done by using a local phone connection to Western Union and a small monthly charge for the use of the satellite. In another situation, I found that I could use strategic allies in other markets to represent my firm's products and services, thereby avoiding costs for expanding to other markets. This reduction in cost allowed us to attract customers who wouldn't have been interested in the higher pricing that would have been necessary with the higher cost structures.

- **Cost to market:** Marketing costs can easily represent 50 percent of a product's cost. Finding the most efficient means to distribute and promote the product or service can provide a real competitive advantage in pricing. Grassroots marketing through local community groups has provided some firms a way of introducing products to key individuals who become fans and product promoters.

- **Funding for operations:** One of the drawbacks to pricing a product based on its direct costs of labor and materials is the inability to properly consider the cost of ongoing administrative, manufacturing, and support operations. Here the lack of understanding costs can result in charging a price for a product that does not cover the associated increase in administrative costs, repair, and maintenance or capital expenditures. One solution is to include an overhead cost factor into the direct-cost calculations for each product.

- **Market positioning:** It is important to remember that the price can suggest value to the consumer. Priced too low a product can be viewed as poor quality and limited value. High pricing can support the image of high-quality product for discerning customers if all of the other marketing components are aligned properly.

- **Availability:** An important consideration in pricing is the availability of the product or service and the ability to find substitutes. If there are markets that do not have easy access to products, then a premium pricing strategy can be employed. Retailers routinely have higher markups in rural areas where competition and product variety are limited.

Product pricing can be critical to a product and ultimately a company's ability to survive and succeed. Approaching pricing as a minor marketing tool can be dangerous.

Reacting to the Competition

Basing price on a competitor's pricing approach is fraught with hazards.

I have worked in several industries and found that pricing is often overlooked as a key marketing tool. In many instances, pricing is driven by the sales department and is a reaction to the competition. This reaction assumes the competition knows the market better and has a superior marketing strategy.

When reacting to the competition it is important to understand that you are being drawn into a game whereby you play by the competitor's rules. You are playing their game and changing your strategy. Your hope here is that you can play the game better or that the competitors can't play their own game very well.

I am reminded of a time where my company was vying for the business of a key customer. The customer was a shrewd negotiator. We understood the value of the customer but valued profit and the perception that our product commanded a higher price. The customer, we knew, would use the price bids to play the competitors against each other.

Our belief was that this was a no-win strategy and decided to bid the price to the point where we would make very little profit and then let the competitor win the bid. We felt that winning the bid was the end game for our competitor and we took the risk that they would lower the price until they won the contract.

Fortunately, we were right; the competition won the contract but couldn't provide the needed level of service. The customer ultimately canceled the contract with the competitor and chose to pay our price for our product. As a result, we were able to service the account and make a profit.

If we had chosen to win the contract, thereby adopting the competitor's strategy we would have lost money, possibly hurt relations with our good customers who were willing to pay a reasonable price for a good product, and earned a reputation as a company that placed short-term market share gain over long-term success.

Pricing to Increase Volume

Lowering price to increase sales volumes can have an adverse effect on the overall marketing strategy.

Pricing can be driven by financial need and the belief that dropping prices will increase sales volume and profitability. This approach is based on the belief that the product has positive price elasticity. Positive price elasticity holds that as prices drop demand increases enough to ensure that the lower margin per unit sold is offset by increased sales volume to the extent that overall profit actually increases.

Using reductions in price to increase volume usually works for a commoditized product that has wide use. This approach usually fails if the product is designed for a specialized use or if the marketing strategy is designed to differentiate the product from others in the marketplace. For differentiated products, the volumes and profits might increase with a price reduction but the value of the efforts to differentiate the product is lost.

Pricing Based on Direct Costs

Marking up a product based on its direct cost may not capture the full value of the product.

Pricing can be based on the information provided by cost accounting that if variable or direct costs are covered then profits can be made. This is indeed valuable information but pricing based on direct costs only concerns itself with the costs of direct materials and labor to produce the product. This strategy is often used when adding a new product to the product mix and is influenced by the need to give the new product every opportunity to succeed.

It also heroically assumes that the established product mix covers fixed costs. This assumption doesn't account for subtle increases that are difficult to measure such as repair and maintenance costs and administrative costs, which are usually considered as fixed.

Pricing a New Product

At one point, I was chairing a new products committee that had developed a new product that had a great deal of promise. The competing products in the market used different production processes and the pricing was significantly higher than was needed to cover our direct costs.

There were several on the committee who suggested that our pricing be just above our direct costs which would, theoretically, allow us to quickly capture the market.

It is important to recognize that customers do not adopt new products based on price particularly if they are satisfied with the results they receive from the products they currently purchase. I argued that a significantly lower price would not recognize the organizational expense and overhead and could possibly suggest to our customers that our product was not equal to the competition since price is often associated with value.

We chose the higher pricing strategy because we felt our product was superior to that of the competition. It took several years to fully penetrate the market but eventually we did capture the market and enjoyed significant sales and profit levels.

If we had adopted the direct-cost pricing model we would have been unable to afford the customer training and interface that was required to have a successful product launch. We also would have been unable to weather the time it took to penetrate the market. The customer training and interface costs were not apparent in the planning phase of the new product and were not considered in the direct-cost model.

Without adoption by the customers the product would have been labeled a loser and dropped from the product offerings. If the direct-cost model had been used and the quality reduced to allow for customer training costs, the customer adoption would have been more problematic because there would have been less differentiation from the product already in use by customers.

Because the pricing strategy was based on value, the product never showed a loss using fully allocated costing models and, in the end, this product captured the market and for years has been a major source of revenue and profit streams.

Using Industry Norms for Pricing

Understanding industry-pricing norms is critical when entering a new line of business.

Houston Chronicle Commercial *Printing Pricing*

The *Houston Chronicle* bought a commercial printing plant and routinely sold printing to their advertisers. The printing was primarily circulars that were inserted into newspapers. The *Chronicle* focused on selling large production runs to large advertisers.

Newspapers typically charge advertisers for space and color when they place an ad in the newspaper. Creating the ad and production work prior to publishing the ad is generally considered part of the cost of the ad and advertisers do not receive an extra charge for this work.

Commercial printers however routinely charge for any work preparing a piece for printing. They charge for artwork, color separations, and prepress work.

The *Chronicle* had moved into the commercial printing arena but had failed to adopt the commercial printing revenue model. As a result the *Chronicle's* commercial printing was not very profitable.

When I joined the *Chronicle*, I was reviewing financial records on a major advertiser's commercial printing work and found that there were no charges for any color or production work. I then met with the customer and said that we would begin charging for these services. The customer was aware of commercial printing costs and accepted the new charges without hesitation.

The lesson here is that when a firm decides to create a new revenue stream it is a good idea to understand how the revenue streams are created to make certain that money isn't left on the table.

Pricing to Increase Revenue Streams

It is important to understand how manufacturing capabilities can provide multiple pricing strategies.

Houston Chronicle ChronDirect Pricing Strategy

The *ChronDirect* program created at the *Houston Chronicle* that combined newspaper delivery with mail delivery of ad circulars required a detailed understanding of how mail costs varied with the type of delivery. To be competitive with other marriage mail programs, the *Chronicle* had to make use of the same postal rates and earn the same discounts.

Marriage mail programs utilized saturation mail meaning that the mail packages went to all households on a mail delivery route. The *Chronicle* would be mailing only to households that did not receive the newspaper.

Because marriage mail went to every household, the mail packages were not addressed but accompanied by a card with the address. This allowed the mail carrier to have a stack of ad packages that could be placed in any mailbox because all households received the same package. This also meant that under that mail program the marriage mail programs could not customize ad packages for delivery to different households.

We found that by addressing the mail in carrier delivery sequence we could match the postal discounts given to the competition plus meet the requirement that we have every address, newspaper subscriber, and non-newspaper subscriber in carrier delivery sequence in our database. While this was a bit more cumbersome, it allowed us to cross-reference various databases with household addresses and provide customized mail packages for advertisers. For example, we were able to cross-reference home ownership and provide a roofing company with addresses of home-owners who had held the same address for 10 or more years.

The *Chronicle* had mail-packaging machinery that could be pro-grammed to assemble marriage mail and newspaper circular packages by address. That is, each address could have a different set of ads based on demographics. The piece mail cost of delivering these packages would be the same as for marriage mail companies delivering a noncustomized saturation mail product to each address.

For pricing purposes, it provided an opportunity for the *Chronicle* to provide normal saturation rates for delivering undifferentiated packages and to charge a premium for custom packages.

The customized product became so popular that at one point a grocer was delivering 96 different versions of their weekly circular to different neighborhoods in Houston.

Pricing to Eliminate Confusion

Eliminating confusing aspects of product pricing can improve market acceptance.

The Houston Chronicle ThisWeek *Pricing Strategy*

The *Houston Chronicle* created a series of local community newspapers (*ThisWeek*) to serve the different city and suburban neighborhoods.

The pricing for these products compared to competing neighborhood newspapers. Usually these newspapers based their pricing on the number of copies delivered in the community since the newspapers were delivered free to every residence.

The *Chronicle* delivered its product to all residences as well. Subscribers received the community newspaper as a section of the *Chronicle* and the nonsubscribers received the community newspaper as a separate newspaper thrown in their yard.

The *Chronicle* had a different advertising rate for each community newspaper but offered a combination rate when an ad was purchased in three or more community newspapers.

The ad rates for each newspaper could vary significantly, and it was cumbersome for ad sales reps to sell ads at the different rates. After some study of sales records, it was noted that most of the reps had sidestepped the varying newspaper rates by selling several community newspaper ads in order to get the bundled rate.

The *Chronicle* then streamlined the system so that an ad in any community newspaper could be purchased for the same rate. This had the benefit of making the sales effort less complicated, the billing and accounting easier to accomplish and understand, and improving sales volume and profit margins.

Bundled Pricing to Increase Sales

Bundled pricing is an excellent way to increase sales volume, create a stronger relationship with customers, and provide a barrier to competitors.

The most viable market for a new product offering is a firm's established customer base. The sales relationship already exists and there is trust between the customer and the firm. A new product introduced by the firm will receive the benefit of this relationship but there may need to be an additional incentive for customers to purchase the new product. One approach is to provide a discount for the new product or existing product, or both, when there is a combined purchase. Insurance companies, Internet, and telecommunications companies, to name a few, use this approach.

This approach has the added benefit of discouraging customers from switching to competing brands since the customer would lose a discount and the competitor would find it difficult to match the discount with just one product.

Houston Chronicle *and ADVO Bundled Pricing*

At the *Houston Chronicle*, there were several categories of customers who spent the majority of their ad budgets with ADVO, a direct mail company that delivered the retailer's mail circulars. ADVO offered very low rates for the very large advertisers by bundling their rates for the Houston market with other markets where the retailers operated.

To counter the multicity discounts offered by ADVO, we offered a discount when a retailer combined their in-newspaper advertising with our circular distribution and our commercial printing of the circulars. The printing discount proved to be key because the *Chronicle* could print for all of the retailer's markets and the printing discount could offset lost ADVO distribution discounts in other markets.

This strategy allowed the *Chronicle* to become a real marketing partner with the retailers. The relationships grew in several cases to the point that the *Chronicle* provided advice and a full array of marketing support programs including digital photography, graphic production consulting, and sales training.

Conclusion

The importance of pricing can be lost when faced with aggressive competition, financial challenges, or a changing industry landscape but it is important to remember that pricing can be as important as any marketing strategy employed when positioning your company.

For a marketing strategist, it is important to consider the vision and mission of the organization. A vision of high quality and customer service will affect pricing strategy differently than an organization with a low-price, self-serve orientation.

It is important to understand that pricing does not stand alone from the other elements of marketing such as product design, distribution, and promotion but rather pricing helps define the value of those attributes.

Revenues and profits that could be realized by unique design, distribution, and promotion based on quality can be lost when the pricing strategy is poorly employed.

CHAPTER 11

Place

The organization's vision and mission must also drive location and distribution strategies. Amazon.com's desire to make customer purchases easy with rapid fulfillment has led Amazon to establish 80 distribution centers and suggest the use of drone aircraft for product delivery.

Finding the right place means providing the customer the right product at the time that is in keeping with the time the customer is willing to invest in searching for the product.

Where should the product be available to maximize sales and profits? Answering this question will have a large impact on a firm's ability to succeed. Again, if research is conducted on the targeted audience using the consumer adoption drivers (CADs) discussed in the chapter on products and services, then a better understanding of the importance of place in the overall marketing strategy can be determined.

For example, search time intensity (STI), if scored low, suggests that customers are not willing to spend a lot of time to find the right product or the best price. This would indicate that convenience is very important. Products fitting in this category can be banking services or items sold at corner convenience stores. If STI scores high, then customers are willing to spend more time searching for the right product or price and convenience is less important.

Locating the Right Place on the Internet

With the advent of the Internet, the ability to make products and services available to targeted markets has been improved. Even so businesses operating on the Internet still must make it easy for the targeted customer base to locate the enterprise and make it easy to conduct business. And some products, due to other CAD factors do not lend themselves to Internet marketing.

The first Internet requirement of making the business easy to locate requires an understanding of the job the customer is hiring the business to perform. The better this is understood the easier it will be to identify keywords that can be used in search engines. For most companies' products, the keywords that can be used are numerous because the products have many different uses. A clothing retailer might use key search words like clothing, dress for success, evening wear, formal wear, casual clothes, latest fashions, and so on.

The second Internet requirement of making it easy to conduct business requires basic market research. To make the Internet site customer friendly, it is necessary to spend time understanding the customers and perhaps walking in their shoes.

Easy Interaction Is a Component of Placement Strategy

Whether it is getting into or out of a parking lot or easily conducting business on the Internet, ease of customer interaction is critical.

Most of us have been to a website or tried to use an automated telephone program that was nothing but frustrating. I can recall a circulation automated customer service program installed at the *Houston Chronicle*. The system allowed individuals to start and stop subscription service and ask for redelivery of missed newspapers. I decided to use the system one day to see how it worked. The program was fairly straightforward and was focused on saving manpower costs, not serving customers. For example, if a customer wanted to stop delivery the system noted the customer's name and account number and proceeded to stop delivery.

It didn't allow a customer to identify problems or seek solutions. It excelled at ending business relationships.

From a marketer's point of view, a customer wishing to end a business relationship is a person to talk to. This is an opportunity to determine whether there were problems with the product or service.

In this case, I changed the system to send customers wishing to stop delivery directly to a senior customer service specialist. This allowed us to determine whether there was a problem that we could act on immediately and whether there was something we could do to save this customer.

Customer Traffic Origination Can Affect Marketing Strategy

For businesses wishing to use the Internet, it is important to understand why a customer would use a website to conduct business and then design the website around the customer's needs.

Understanding SFGate *Web Traffic Data*

The *San Francisco Chronicle's* website is *SFGate*. The managers of *SFGate* regularly reported that their unique visitors were higher than almost all other newspapers in the United States. This concerned me a bit because the site was generating small revenues and no profit.

A little investigation revealed the reason there were so many visitors to the site was due to the popularity of San Francisco as a travel destination and *SFGate* regularly came to the top of the search list when San Francisco was queried on the Internet search engines. Unfortunately this traffic did not provide a means of generating robust revenues.

Further investigation allowed us to understand what was important to people in the Bay Area who regularly used the Internet. To increase revenues we had to develop programs of interest for individuals in the Bay Area. We found that entertainment, wine, food, and classified listings were of interest. With the proper focus, we were able to significantly improve the traffic from individuals living in the Bay Area.

While Internet commerce continues to grow, there are however, many instances where a business manager must pay particular attention to the physical location business outlets.

Physical Locations

Convenience still plays a critical role in physical location for businesses such as restaurants, banks, and grocery stores.

HEB Location Strategy

HEB Grocery Company is a privately owned chain of grocery stores operating in Texas and Mexico. The firm is just over 100 years old and is the dominant grocer in a large portion of Texas.

HEB faced competition from a large number of local and national grocery chains in central and south Texas. A&P, Kroger, Safeway, and Albertson's were the primary national chains in these areas.

In Texas, there has been significant economic growth. Neighborhood demographics have changed and new suburbs continue to be developed.

Recognizing the market shifts, HEB closed old stores in many neighborhoods and replaced them with newer facilities and opened new stores in the growing suburban areas. The new stores offered the latest features such as delis, in-store bakeries and expanded general merchandise offerings. Additionally the new stores offered features that matched with the neighborhood demographics.

The major chains competing in the same markets, for the most part, did not build or relocate their stores to accommodate the changes in the marketplace. As a result, at least in part, A&P, Safeway, Kroger, and Albertson's no longer have any operations in south and central Texas. Today this area is completely dominated by HEB Grocery Company.

HEB continues to review and revitalize store locations to recognize individual neighborhood demographics. This process has helped maintain market leadership.

Using Established Networks to Reach Key Markets at American Property Data

American Property Data (APD) was a company founded with the idea that new approaches to helping investors locate prime commercial property could improve the efficacy of the commercial real estate industry.

The key to making the APD system work was to have prime commercial real estate as part of the system's inventory. This inventory would attract quality real estate investors. Matching key investors with properties that fit their investing profiles would attract more property and provide a solid revenue stream.

Since most of the prime commercial real estate was located in large metropolitan markets and represented by successful commercial real estate brokers, it was important to have key commercial brokers in key markets enter their real estate inventories into the APD system.

To attract these brokers, APD offered market exclusivity. The APD affiliate in the market would have access to APD inventory across the country as well as key investors that subscribed to the APD services.

This approach proved successful, and in about 2 years, APD grew to have representation in most major cities in the United States.

Logistics

If the physical location is convenient and the website is easy to find and friendly, it is all lost if the customer is unable to have access to the needed products.

Inventory and logistics planning is a critical component of execution management. Developing strong relationships with suppliers and understanding product inventory requirements are crucial.

Amazon clearly has one of the customer friendliest websites on the Internet. To make certain that customers receive the merchandise as soon as possible, Amazon has created a network of distribution centers nationwide.

Walmart and Target are developing strategies to compete with Amazon.com by combining friendly websites with store distribution capabilities.

The place P of marketing is continuing to evolve as the Internet makes products and services more accessible to consumers. The forms that will have the greatest success are those that can combine product fulfillment with Internet accessibility and involve the customer in the shopping experience through the physical location or the Internet.

PART III

Implementation

This section of the book will focus on the processes and programs to be used when developing tactics to be carried out after the price, place, product, and promotion strategies have been developed.

CHAPTER 12

A Process for Execution Management

I can remember early in my career when I was asked to manage a department that was disorganized and not meeting its organizational objectives. While somewhat flattered, I was also afraid that I wouldn't be successful. I didn't have experience in defining organizational problems or developing their solutions. In this particular case, I just decided to take an action and see where it led. As luck would have it, the early actions raised questions that would require that I do some research into how others had dealt with similar problems.

In most cases, the research gave good pointers on how to move forward and what next steps might produce results. The next steps usually led to more questions that required further research that led to still more steps to be taken.

While this approach moved the project forward, it didn't provide a list of activities that would focus on improving the department's ability to function effectively. This approach almost required that I discover problems and inconsistencies as I tried to implement changes.

There are a lot of great ideas for new business initiatives and new businesses. There are also established businesses that must make changes in their organizations to grow or even to survive. The difference between a needed outcome and achieving that outcome is in execution.

Execution is the process of taking something from an idea to a completed project. This usually boils down to attention to detail. It requires breaking a needed outcome into components that can be described and measured.

I have found that the best process starts with a clear definition of the needed outcome. Once the outcome was defined, a review of all of the steps needed to achieve that outcome helped identify actions that were needed. This allowed the development of an execution plan rather than discovering needed actions during an implementation effort.

If the components of a project's envisioned outcome are specific enough, then a plan can be developed. The plan must be specific and detailed enough to completely implement the envisioned initiative.

The plan must consider all aspects of an initiative: environment, economy, competition, resources required, coordination of marketing strategy with management capabilities, and so on.

Here are some steps using an end-to-beginning planning process to improve the level of execution success.

1. **Planning:** When setting a plan, envision the end result; then take this vision and begin working backward to the beginning of the project. If the vision is to open a retail outlet, envision the store, the customers, the location, the merchandise, the fixtures and layout, your income (or profit), the employees and their level of expertise, and so on.

Each of these envisioned characteristics requires specific actions. For example, if an upscale location is envisioned, then identifying acceptable sites, rents, build-out requirements, and lease terms are required action items.

Envisioned profit levels will require a certain sales volume, pricing strategy, and marketing effort. The staffing quality will come at a certain level of payroll and benefit expense. The actions here will help in developing the strategy for the initiative.

2. **List of action items:** The action items for each characteristic should be listed in a sequential format. For example, one would need to identify a location before considering build-out requirements. The sequence of action items once laid out should be set to a specific timetable. Thus if opening a retail outlet is envisioned to take place in 6 months, the identification of an acceptable outlet would have to take place and leave enough time to negotiate lease terms, build out, install fixtures, and take inventory.

At his stage, the planner may find that there are conflicts that require resolution. In this example, if the build-out requires 4 months and fixtures have a 5-month lead time, adjustments will have to be made in the time line. It may require setting a different opening date or finding ways to order fixtures before build-out activities begin. This is where the use of a critical path or program evaluation review technique (PERT) chart would be useful. Mind Tools provides a good tutorial for using the critical path method and PERT at www.mindtools.com/critpath.html

There may also be strategic conflicts. For example, if the end-to-beginning analysis uncovers competitive, legal, or other potential roadblocks, additional strategic planning may be required.

3. **Assign specific action items and timetables to individual managers:** This allows each activity to be tracked by a responsible individual. This individual can alert others when difficulties are encountered so that actions can be taken to keep the whole project on schedule.

This approach allows the identification of the final objective and a means of analyzing all aspects of the project in the planning stage rather than in the execution stage. It also helps uncover inconsistencies in strategic planning.

Once the actions necessary for implementation are consistent with the organization's vision, the activities are arranged in the most efficient sequence and assigned to responsible individuals for follow-through. With a solid plan that defines time lines and assigned responsibilities, a manager is in a position for the successful execution of a project.

CHAPTER 13

Organizational Structure

Implementing tactics to support vision driven strategies will require an organization built around organizational goals. This chapter focuses on organizational development for strategic success.

Five Steps to Building an Organization That Achieves Goals

Effective implementation of marketing strategy and tactics requires an effective organization to carry out the tasks.

One of the most satisfying experiences I have had is building a workforce that is focused on achieving and exceeding organizational goals. I have found that taking five steps can have a significant impact on this process. The five steps are as follows:

- **Design the organization and workforce structure around the goals of the organization:** This is more easily accomplished if you are starting a new business and more difficult for older and more established businesses. It is helpful to envision an organization successfully meeting its goals and think about the structure and employees driving that organization. Those goals can be making a certain level of profit, reaching a certain market segment, being a market leader, providing a certain level of service, and so on. Many businesses may have all of the aforementioned and more as stated goals. With these goals in mind, it is important then to look at the organization's functional components, finance, sales and marketing, production, distribution, and research and development, and make certain their goals are aligned with the organization's goals. For example, having an organizational goal of meeting customers' specialized needs will face difficulty if the production arm of the organization is focused on cost control. Here, the production goal might be restated to find the most efficient method of fulfilling customers' needs. Sales and marketing in this instance would need to focus on working with customers to find solutions that efficiently meet their needs. This allows the organization to strive to meet the customers' specialized needs while providing efficiently designed customer solutions to the production department. This will almost always require open communication channels between the organization's functional components.

- **Clearly articulate goals**: Beginning with the hiring process, keep the organization's goals in mind. If the organization is structured properly, then the workforce positions in each of the functional components will support the overall organizational goals. In the previous example, marketing secretaries will understand the kinds of services being offered and know how to direct traffic to the right marketing individual. Production personnel will constantly be on the lookout for more efficient methods to produce quality outcomes. Accountants will focus on tracking costs and providing information to improve the organization's ability to provide the best service competitively while generating acceptable profit levels.

- **Design training around organizational goals:** Training new employees and retraining long-term employees will have to be focused on meeting organizational goals. Here customer focus is very important. If employees can see how they fit into a process that successfully addresses a customer's needs, then they are more likely to be engaged reaching organizational goals. I have been involved in an organization that was large and well established but operated on internal departmental goals that built resentment and reduced cooperation between departments. By changing the organization's focus to the customer, we improved interdepartmental communication, efficiency, customer satisfaction, and profits.

- **Design pay and bonus structures around organizational goals:** Pay and incentive programs should be designed to achieve organizational goals. Using the previous example, if production personnel were rewarded on low cost per item produced and sales and marketing were rewarded for market share improvement and the overall organizational goals were to meet customers' specialized needs, there would likely be friction between departments and dissatisfied customers. On the other hand, if both departments were rewarded for achieving market share growth and improved profitability, then the organization and the customer are more likely to be successful.

- **Be careful about adding new jobs and new functions:** Every new job or organizational function should be evaluated on its ability to help the organization achieve its goals. Executives and department managers can be very persuasive when requesting additional resources. It is important to use organizational goals as the metric to determine the need for the additional resources.

- **Develop extracurricular activities to support organizational goals:** When developing programs to engage personnel and build relationships with customers, it is important to keep organizational goals in mind. It will be hard for employees or customers to see how lavish parties promote efficiency. On the other hand, well thought-out social events can build relationships that foster good customer relations and employee morale and focus.

The aforementioned process is fairly simple but requires daily focus. I have found that when orchestrated properly, it results in an organization that routinely exceeds expectations, customers who are satisfied, and a workforce that is self-directed and motivated.

Organizational Structures for a New Business

I have recently been involved in two start-ups that may prove as useful examples for a less structured, more evolutionary approach for developing organizational structures.

The first is a collaboration between Rice University, MD Anderson Cancer Center, and the National Space Biomedical Research Institute. The job to be done is to create and commercialize devices for delivery of health care at a distance. The focus is on cancer prevention and care. The organization is known as the eHealth Research Institute.

As it turns out, the steps following the identification of the job to be done and the development of a vision statement may be more evolutionary than taking clearly identified methodical steps. For example, in a recent planning session, we were considering the various organizational structures that might be adopted. The best structure would be one that allowed continued support from the founding institutions while allowing the ability to attract public and private funding for the new organization.

While the direction follows my recommended approach, it differs in the ability to easily identify a clear strategic plan. The reason is the potential for environmental change. The potential for change in funding from the current public and private sources has to be considered as well as the potential for change in focus for the founding institutions.

We believe the new devices that will be created for commercialization by the eHealth Research Institute have the ability to change health care delivery worldwide. To be successful, we will have to have a means of attracting the best projects into the institute that can be moved to the prototype stage; then we will have to find funding to support research while the projects are being moved to the final stages of development. We will have to rely on grants and philanthropic funding for the initial stages of the projects; then we will have to create partnerships with venture capitalists, private investors, and corporations to move the devices from prototype stages to commercialization.

This organizational process will have to be evolutionary in nature. There are examples we can draw upon for guidance but this organization will be different enough from others that it will require innovation and the ability to adapt to a changing environment. A list of activities to be accomplished will be necessary to develop the organization but rather than each step leading to a clearly definable next step, it will likely lead to a series of options that will require some research before making a choice. It may be that the organization will be different than that which we envision today.

Another example is a consulting venture that I am participating in. In this case, it is pretty clear that our firm will be consulting on infrastructure development in a Central American country. This will be the first such project for our consulting firm and will be the foundation for similar projects in other countries. We believe we are the preferred vendor because our expertise in this area is second to none.

The challenge here is developing an organization that that can grow very rapidly and maintain the quality of service. The good news is that we have access to a large pool of qualified experts and we are very good at identifying what must be done to successfully complete each project.

In this case, we initially proposed on working on one project but we have been asked to provide guidance on all similar type projects. This was a growth in the potential size of the project and it comes at a time when another country is considering our services for a similar type of engagement.

Here the potential organizational solutions will not be easily identifiable but will rather look like a decision tree, each branch offering a different probability of success or outcome.

In both examples, the development of the organization is evolutionary in nature and the outcomes cannot be easily predicted. This makes planning, financial and otherwise, more difficult.

To remove some of the ambiguity, it is best not to engage in long-term planning. It is probably better to identify the next decision point and plan to successfully operate through that decision.

For example, with the eHealth Research Institute if we can identify a means of raising enough financial support to move us forward on identifying and attracting four to five projects for development without finalizing the ultimate organizational structure, then we have a short-term win and the ability to better study the next organizational decision. We have identified one research organization that has been successful that took 6 years before reaching its current organization structure.

For the consulting firm, the organizational structure will develop based on the types of demands placed on the organization. Strategic alliances may be critical for success in the short run then economics or other criteria may require developing a larger internal staff.

Build Your Business by Forming Alliances

How do you grow a business to take when you simply don't have the resources to focus on new opportunities? How do you attract new talent that can bring new business without adding a financial burden to your organization?

Forming business alliances is an approach that is being used today to meet these challenges.

Retail Opportunities

A major retail grocery chain uses an alliance to provide sushi bars in its retail stores. The grocer contacted a small sushi catering service and asked whether the caterer would be interested in finding individuals to set up sushi bars in the retail stores. In return the grocer would use its buying power to provide sushi ingredients at the lowest possible rate and keep track of sales through its registers. Further the grocery company would subtract the cost of goods sold and simply pay the caterer a percentage of the profit of each sushi item sold.

The caterer found a source of individuals willing to set up and man the sushi bars in the grocery stores by forming a subcontractor arrangement. Essentially the caterer provides training and quality control to the subcontractor for each store and shares the money from sales with the subcontractor.

The results have been very significant. The grocer has sushi bars in 200 outlets and is very happy with the product quality, sales volume, and customer service the caterer has provided. This was accomplished without having to hire new employees or other expenses associated with adding a new service to the grocery operation.

The caterer was able to expand his business without taking on additional financial risk and the business has been so successful that he has a waiting list of quality subcontractors to start sushi bars in grocery stores.

This program has been so successful that the grocer is now looking at other services that can be added to the retail outlet using the same model.

Consulting Service Opportunities

A well-established accounting firm wanted to expand its consulting business without increasing the costs associated with attracting high-powered consultants from a wide range of industries. The consulting firm created teaming agreements that allowed small consulting firms to work with the larger firm.

The small consulting firm would have the ability to offer a full line of consulting services and would be supported by the larger consulting firm's staff. The larger consulting firm would have the benefit of the smaller consulting firm's contacts, relationships, and new business opportunities.

As a result, the smaller consultants were able to call on major clients and offer services without taking on additional cost for expanded support staff. The larger consulting firm, as a result, generated more sales and had the expertise of consultants from a myriad of industries without the associated employment costs.

Technology Sales Opportunities

A technology company that provides groundbreaking teleconferencing display hardware uses relationships with technology sales organizations to market their products. The technology company is able to reach new markets and customers by tapping into the sales organization's contacts and established relationships.

The sales organization's ability to offer its clients the latest in teleconferencing hardware enhances its ability to create new revenue streams.

As a result, the technology company has had its equipment exposed to new industries and is experiencing strong sales growth.

Steps to Creating Successful Business Alliances

To create a successful business alliance, all partners must benefit. Here is a checklist to follow when considering forming a business alliance.

1. Make certain the partner has the skill sets and ability to deliver agreed upon goods or services. A test project may help determine each party's capabilities prior to forming a long-term relationship.

2. Be sure to clearly define each party's responsibilities and obligations at the outset of the relationship. This should be a written document that covers normal operating procedures, revenue and expense allocations, and how out-of-the-normal situations will be handled. The ability for each party to end the relationship should be agreed upon in writing.

3. Develop a business strategy. A plan should be designed that shows how each member of the alliance will benefit and outlines their role in creating business opportunities that benefit all alliance members.

4. Set regular meetings with alliance partners. Meetings should be held regularly to review the progress toward achieving desired results and to discuss new programs and opportunities.

5. Terminate the alliance if it is not working. Everyone hopes for success in a newly formed alliance but there will be some alliances that will not be productive. It is better to terminate a program that isn't working rather than continue putting effort and resources in an unworkable program.

As the global economy expands, building business alliances will become an important tool to create and develop new business opportunities. Choosing the right partners and alliance operating procedures can improve the chances the alliances will have a successful outcome.

Conclusion

This chapter has focused on organizational development that promotes strategic success by building strategic objectives into the structure and muscle of the organization. We also discuss the instances where it is better to let the organizational structure evolve as allowed by the environment and how to use alliances to build an organization when appropriate.

CHAPTER 14

Workforce

Much like organizational development, the design of the workforce is critical to effective implementation of vision and mission driven strategies.

Tie Culture Change to Business Outcomes

As a manager, you may find that your organization has flaws that are hampering performance. These flaws may have become a hardwired part of the organization's culture and to move the organization forward you need to shift or remake the culture.

Larry Bossidy, former chairman of Honeywell International, writes that most organizations' attempts to change culture fail because they are not tied to improving business outcomes.

Culture is the result of management practices and philosophy that is developed over time. Everyone in the organization knows the culture and most abide by the attitudes and approaches that define the path to success in the organization.

I can recall working in a very successful, very large newspaper organization that was entering into the commercial printing business. They were making some headway but not the kind of growth they had envisioned.

The newspaper was located in a big city and the commercial printing opportunities were significant. One challenge was the presses owned by the newspaper. The presses that printed the newspaper used the letterpress process, which didn't produce the quality provided by the offset process used by commercial printers. To address this, the newspaper purchased a printing company that had heat-set offset printing presses. This not only provided offset printing; it allowed even higher (near magazine) quality printing.

While this provided an advantage, this printing press was only economically viable for large press runs. This limited the ability to sell smaller print jobs. To address this, the newspaper used smaller commercial printers to print the jobs sold by the newspaper's sales staff.

This is where culture got in the way. The newspaper had an approved list of two or three outside printing vendors that could be used. These printers had long-standing relationships with the newspaper. Their prices were well above market prices, thereby limiting the sales to those in desperate need or who were not knowledgeable of printing prices. At times, the newspaper would bundle advertising with printing and discount the advertising to offset cost of the printing. Since the newspaper was the primary advertising vehicle at the time, this approach generated a respectable amount of revenue but provided less profit than just selling advertising.

This approach was the result of a culture that emphasized the newspaper's leadership position in the marketplace. Basically, it said to staff and ultimately to the market that the newspaper set the rules, not the marketplace. All too often a request made by a customer was simply turned away due to lack of capacity or inability to meet the customer's needs.

There is a huge chasm between identifying the need for a cultural shift and actually causing a cultural shift. We knew we needed to change because there was a lot of business that was going to competitors. We were primarily concerned with winning back grocery advertisers that used to insert their circulars in the newspaper but had moved to the mail. In doing so, grocers had found printing vendors would give them high-quality printing, low prices, and good production support. To move forward, we would have to significantly change our culture to one that was focused on the customer.

Clearly, the only way we were going to change culture was to have a significantly positive business outcome directly related to a change favoring a focus on customer service.

Effectively dealing with this issue meant convincing management that if we focused on the customer, we could increase revenues and profits. To do this meant that we would have to open the doors to outside printers and let them compete for our business. We would choose those printing vendors that provided the best pricing and the best service.

Convincing management was not easy. Their view was that they understood what was needed and that competing against every printer in the marketplace would drive down prices and overall profit. Their defense was good, the newspaper was very successful, and there was no need to fix that, which was not broken.

We were fortunate that circumstances arose that allowed us to test the water a bit. We sold a very large contract that required the use of new outside services. A vice president showed his displeasure and lobbied to use the old approach. Using the old approach however, would mean cancelling a very profitable, multimillion-dollar contract. It was ultimately decided that it was in the company's best interest to fulfill the contract. This opened the door to try this approach on several other advertisers.

Over the next year or so, our commercial printing revenues doubled and our profits improved at an even higher rate. More importantly, we were able to position ourselves as a provider that could meet virtually any printing need.

As an example, late one Monday morning we received a frantic call from one of our largest advertisers that they needed a circular delivered by mail and it needed to be in consumers' mailboxes by that Thursday. We said that it wouldn't be a problem, just tell us where we needed to pick up the circulars and we would deliver them to the post office.

She told us that the circulars hadn't been printed. We said it might be a little more difficult but we would drop by and pick up the artwork. She then told us that the artwork wasn't ready. Further, when we sent a production manager to collect materials as they were produced we found that scanning the artwork was slowing down the process.

The production manager called one of the printing vendors and alerted them of the situation. Scanning was dropped in favor of a flatbed camera. This and a few other production process changes allowed us to get the customers' circular into their mailboxes on that Thursday.

This kind of service led to the ability to advise customers on all of their advertising and ad production needs. We found ourselves providing photography services, digital imaging services, and direct mail services.

By tying the needed change directly to business outcomes, the newspaper was able to change its culture from one focused on past practices to one focused on customer needs.

Cross-Functional Teams

Changing organizational culture needs to be tied to business outcomes to be successful; an approach to implement organizational culture is through using cross-functional teams.

Culture change may be necessary for organizations to adapt to changing environments. If old value networks (processes, procedures, communication channels, and protocols) govern, then survival in a changing marketplace becomes more difficult.

This is a dilemma that is the result of dated value networks becoming part of a hardwired approach to problem solving within the industry. These are hardwired in the sense that they are part of the culture and very difficult to change.

Most companies require innovations to create new revenue and profit streams for growth and long-term success. Innovation is needed for developing new products or finding new markets for current products. Either approach requires new strategies and is based on innovative thinking. For new ideas to be incorporated into the "muscle" of the organization, it may require a "rewiring" of the organization's culture.

This rewiring requires participation by all of the organization's functional groups (finance, marketing, sales, production, and human resources) and becomes difficult if it is at odds with the hardwired thinking. Rewiring is almost impossible if a new idea is adopted by one organizational function that tries to force the total organization into adopting the new approach.

Cross-Functional Teams at Corpus Christi Caller-Times

Cross-functional teams can provide options to hardwired approaches to problem solving and promote buy-in across the organization.

Beginning with my first assignment to review the market position of the *Corpus Christi Caller-Times* and to make recommendations on actions needed, I looked to a cross-functional task group for solutions. An assignment that might change things across an organization was daunting, and it was clear to me that I did not have enough knowledge of the organization's functions to determine the impact of any potential changes. A task group comprising individuals from across the organization would help combat inertia from hardwired approaches and would allow any new approaches to appreciate organizational constraints, weaknesses, and exploit organizational strengths.

Information presented to the task group showed the market comprised a growing number of small businesses that didn't need and couldn't afford to have their advertising in the newspaper, which was distributed to subscribers across south Texas.

The financial data showed the economics of running the newspaper presses. Because the presses were large and required a significant work group to run, products produced needed to be printed in substantial quantities. This meant a high variable or direct cost and would require significant revenue streams. These revenue streams would not be possible to generate from the growing number of small businesses that wanted to focus on the immediate markets around their business location.

Presented with this information and with some study of what was being done in other markets, the task group suggested that a group of limited circulation products be developed for small businesses. A local commercial printer would print these products on smaller presses. Advertising pricing would be lower due to reduced costs, and distribution would be in several zones. Each zone would cover a specific area of the city where a group of businesses and their potential customers were located.

What was revealing about the task group approach was the immediate buy-in by each of the participants into finding a solution to a business challenge. From this buy-in came real problem solving and the willingness by the representative of each functional group to take recommendations back to their people and discuss how implementation could be achieved. I again think this goes back to some of the theories on human motivation. There was no carrot or threat here; only the creation of a group that provided acceptance, status, and recognition.

In the end, a very successful group of products were introduced. These products allowed the *Caller-Times* to strengthen its market position for years to come.

Cross-Functional Teams at the Houston Chronicle

A program known as marriage mail affected the Houston advertising market. Marriage mail is a program that allows advertisers to combine their advertising circulars in one mail package and share the mail costs. Marriage Mailers, a small direct mail operation in Los Angeles first used the concept. ADVO, a direct marketer established in 1929, bought Marriage Mailers in 1979 and began rolling out the program nationwide.

Until the introduction of marriage mail, advertising circulars were primarily distributed by newspapers and represented a very profitable revenue stream. Newspapers at the time did not feel the need to lower their rates for circular distribution because they felt they had a superior delivery system. Some retailers felt otherwise and began using the marriage mail concept, and over the next 20 years, newspapers lost the majority of grocery inserts to marriage mail.

Houston had become one of ADVO's most profitable markets to the detriment of the *Houston Post* and *Houston Chronicle*. In 1993, I was charged with creating a mail product for the *Houston Chronicle* that would compete with ADVO.

Since the project would require support from across the organization, I decided to create a cross-functional team to put together a response. This team met every Friday morning for the remainder of my tenure at the *Houston Chronicle*. By early 1994, we had created a product that was delivered to newspaper subscribers in the newspaper and to the remainder of the market through the U.S. Postal Service. Due to the mix of delivery, we were able to offer full market coverage at prices less than those offered by ADVO. The program was in full swing across the Houston Market in 1995, and by late 1995 all of the key retailers had abandoned ADVO and moved to the *Chronicle's* program.

The task force met each week to review the prior week's performance and address any new issues that arose. Over the following 7 years the program, which became known as *ChronDirect*, was embellished to allow specific address delivery at marriage mail pricing and demographic and psychographic market delivery programs. The production department determined how to reduce mailing and distribution costs to ensure new entrants would not be able to match the service or the price. Today *ChronDirect* remains the most successful advertising distribution vehicle in the Houston market.

It is clear to me that no individual could have developed and implemented this program. It is also clear to me that cross-functional task groups can provide real employee engagement and job satisfaction while helping the organization grow.

For me, it has been reaffirmed that the ability to change the culture of an organization must be rooted in a focus on a business outcome and implemented by cross-functional teams.

Five Steps to Developing a Strong Workforce

Having a capable workforce is critical to building a successful organization. Here are five steps that can improve the workforce building process.

1. **Screening:** Assembling the right group of individuals for your workforce is important. You can test for competency but being part of a team means that individuals must have personalities that can work together. Assuredly this means that some subjectivity will enter into the screening process. It may also mean that wrong choices will be made and will need correction. The subjectivity and chance for errors can be reduced with the introduction of 10 tips from About .com Human Resources at http://humanresources.about.com/od/ recruiting/tp/recruiting_employee.htm

2. **Defining job responsibilities:** Even with the right personnel, the workforce can be dysfunctional if each member's responsibilities are not clearly defined. It is management's responsibility to understand how each job contributes to the organization's success and to clearly articulate the requirements of each job.

3. **Defining job success:** After each member of the workforce understands the requirements of his or her job, it is important that he or she understands what success looks like. This can be presented in terms of meeting specific deadlines, producing specific results in production or sales or levels of customer satisfaction. It is important for individual members of the organization to understand how success in their job relates to the overall success of the organization.

4. **Establishing metrics:** Favoritism and improperly set work rules can destroy the morale and ultimately the effectiveness of a good workforce. Setting specific metrics for job performance lets individuals know how their performance will be graded. If developed properly,

it will eliminate favoritism and improper work rules. The University of California suggests using the following SMART test to determine the quality of performance metrics.

S = Specific: clear and focused to avoid misinterpretation. Should include measurement assumptions and definitions and be easily interpreted.

M = Measurable: can be quantified and compared to other data. It should allow for meaningful statistical analysis. Avoid "yes/no" measures except in limited cases, such as start-up or systems-in-place situations.

A = Attainable: achievable, reasonable, and credible under conditions expected.

R = Realistic: fits into the organization's constraints and is cost-effective.

T = Timely: doable within the time frame given.

5. **Workforce participation in job design:** Most individuals spend the majority of their time in the workplace. For the highest level of productivity, members of a workforce should feel that they are part of the organization and can have real input into how jobs are designed. The workplace can be a site for individual growth and learning as well as a place to produce goods and services. If individuals understand what is needed for the organization to succeed, participation in job design can lead to higher productivity for the organization and higher morale with lower turnover for the workforce.

Finding People to Accomplish the Extraordinary

Choosing the right individuals to build an organization is critical. When organizational challenges are extraordinary, finding the right people is absolutely essential. The question arises "How do you identify these key individuals?" There is no infallible process but I have had some experiences that might provide some assistance.

I can recall being a new publisher of a community daily newspaper that was experiencing difficulties in the production areas at a time we were also building a new plant, installing new presses, and purchasing new production equipment.

We used recruiters to help us find qualified individuals to place in key production areas as leaders. After a thorough review (we thought) of their background and capabilities and interviews with our corporate leadership, we hired several of the individuals who were recommended.

With this new group of production leaders, the installation of presses and production equipment was disastrous and production problems were worse than when we started. Our newsprint waste percentage was through the roof and we had partial newsprint rolls sitting around the press storage area. I felt like we just could not get our operations in order and my frustration continued to mount.

Then one afternoon I was walking through the production area and noticed a man working on his car in our parking lot. I struck up a conversation with him and learned he was looking for a job. I asked whether he knew anything about newspaper presses. He said he knew newspaper presses and knew how to fix our problems. I was intrigued. I asked how he would deal with the problem of waste and the partial newsprint rolls since we had no newsprint rewinder to combine the rolls.

He said he could rig a rewinder using the press motors and he could significantly reduce the waste caused by the press start-up process. Out of frustration I said if he could clean up and use the partial rolls and reduce the press waste by 50 percent in 6 weeks, the press leadership job was his. He agreed, built a rewinder, reduced the press waste, and became the press foreman.

Similarly, in our prepress area we had waste problems and a miserable record of meeting deadlines required for timely delivery of the newspaper. One day a fellow walked in looking for a job and said he was a prepress manager.

We were shorthanded and I said that I would hire him as foreman on a 6-week trial. On his first afternoon I asked him how things were going and he said, "Just fine, I fired a couple of folks and the process has really improved."

At that newspaper there were two more hires, a circulation manager and a photocomposition supervisor who had similar positive results. These folks, A. J. Roberson (press), Larry Kennedy (prepress), Linda Kelley (photocomposition), and Jimmy Jerkins (circulation), saved the day at that newspaper.

This group loved the challenge, loved the feeling of succeeding, and loved bonding with each other as a winning team. They followed me when I started another newspaper and when I was called in to save a failing newspaper. In every case, they performed at the highest skill level and routinely did what others would have said couldn't be done.

As an example, this group, with modest financial backing, led the effort to start a newspaper from scratch in just 90 days. We started with an announcement of our intent to start a daily newspaper in 90 days and publish from our plant on our presses with our staff. Incredibly, in 90 days we acquired land, built a building, installed presses and production equipment, hired and trained staff, and produced our first of many editions.

Later in my career, I was asked to lead an effort to turn around a major metropolitan newspaper. My friends who helped me build and turn around community newspapers had gone on to other endeavors or had passed away. This job was going to be difficult, so I began interviewing for the key slot, which was the vice president of the advertising division.

There were plenty of applicants, but I needed someone for a very difficult job, so I used an interview approach that would narrow the group down to individuals who really wanted to be in this difficult situation and work with me. In the interview, I painted the situation as a "knife fight in a telephone booth." In other words, if we failed the outcome would not be pretty.

There was one individual who stood out as a person who was energized by the challenge, had all the requisite skills, and impressed me as someone I wanted on my team. His name was Gordon Prouty and he was key in building a team that led the organization to new heights in revenue growth and new product development. Gordy is now publisher of a newspaper and leads his own team successfully.

So if I have advice to offer people building or assessing a team, I would say that their team members should answer two questions.

First ask, "If everything in your world was perfect, what would you be doing today?" If the answer is pretty far removed from being a member of your team addressing the challenges your organization faces, you may have the wrong team member. If it is an applicant you may want to remove him or her from the pool. If it is a current member of your team you may want to consider reassignment or another approach that lessens his or her role. There will be cases where the individual will have to be replaced.

The second question to ask is "Can the challenges facing the organization be successfully addressed in short order?" If the answer is no or that more time is needed you may have identified an individual who should not be on your team or should be reassigned.

The final piece of advice is to you, the leader. I would say that you should answer the question "Am I prepared to make changes in the team based on the responses to the questions asked?"

If you are not willing to take the action, are you really serious about changing the direction of the organization? If the challenge is extraordinary, do you have the team to lead you to success?

Conclusion

This chapter has focused on developing a workforce that is focused on achieving organizational goals. We have discussed how to change culture by focusing on needed outcomes, how to use cross-functional teams to eliminate resistance to needed change and build an organization that is goal oriented, and we have introduced criteria to help managers choose workforce members. Driven by mission and vision, a workforce that is goal driven will provide significant advantages.

CHAPTER 15

Financial Structure and Controls

As discussed in previous chapters, the vision and mission driven strategies for price, place, product, and promotion will have an impact on cash requirements of an organization. This chapter will discuss this impact and provide some examples for consideration.

Six Steps to Developing Low-Cost New Businesses

Starting a new business doesn't necessarily mean that large amounts of money need to be raised. Even businesses with the potential of capturing a new market of substantial size may not require a substantial investment. This may be good news for individuals with a great idea coupled with expertise and know-how.

I have seen individuals lose control of their ideas and their vision of a successful company by seeking out investors to support the company in its early stages. This can be avoided by building the business through alliances and involving individuals who can benefit if the business is a success.

Steps in setting up a low-cost venture should include:

- **Identify potential prospects** who would benefit from the product or service to be offered. These prospects can be interviewed to see whether your offering is going to fill a market need. They may be enlisted to further refine the offering.
- **Once the product or service is validated, find a strategic ally** that is willing to work with you by adding your product to their offerings or by allowing you or include their products to your offerings. This automatically creates market credibility. The more successful your ally the better your credibility.

- **Maintain control of your business:** This can be difficult and dangerous especially if working with a very aggressive business ally. One way of providing control is making sure that business transactions and cash flows are conducted through your company. That is, customers pay you and you pay your business ally.
- **Avoid large administrative and workforce expenditures:** To process payments, payroll, business expenses, insurance, and billing use an accounting service. There will be a fee for these services but there is no organizational expense and the cost of the service is directly related to the level of activity.
- **Find a university business school that is looking for internships for their students:** These students can provide a workforce at a low cost and can be the beginning of permanent staffing and a future management team.
- **Plan an investment strategy** that allows you to seek out investors when you have the best negotiating position.

At the *Houston Chronicle*, we sought out new publications that could be distributed in our newspaper. The publication would help the *Chronicle* reach a broader spectrum of the community. The publication would benefit by having the credibility of being distributed in the *Chronicle* (they were able to command a higher advertising rate) without the cost of an internal distribution organization. *Paper City*, which is now in several major cities started with an alliance with the *Houston Chronicle*. It began as a very small operation and has grown significantly by strategically developing and controlling business alliances.

In a venture currently taking shape, a group of physicians felt that there was a need for a consulting service that provided health care guidance to underdeveloped nations. These doctors visited with several countries and were well received. One country invited the doctors to visit and make a presentation on the development of a major hospital.

The doctors explained the opportunity to a major architectural or engineering firm that had a great deal of experience building hospitals internationally and invited them to be a strategic ally.

The architectural firm accepted the alliance and accompanied the doctors to visit the country's health ministry and make the presentation.

The presentation went very well and the doctors' group is now being considered for consulting services on five hospitals as well as other health ministry programs.

To develop a staff to gather information, the doctors have identified a university with a health care MBA program that is looking for opportunities for their students. The work for the students will be meaningful and cogent to their career objectives. The company will receive bright, capable individuals working on programs to solve health care challenges for the health ministry of a developing nation.

Cash flows for this new health care consulting company will come from regular payments from the contracting government and paid directly to the doctors' consulting firm. The consulting firm, based on services requested, will pay all payments to business allies.

In this case, the consulting company will have significant expenditures only when there is a significant revenue stream. Organizational expenses are held to a minimum and tightly controlled.

Finally, the health care consulting company is developing a long-term strategy to attract investors when they have a strong ongoing business.

Loan Cash to Corporate Operating Units to Improve Cash Flows

In most corporations, the cost of money affects the ability to compete successfully. If money has to be borrowed, then the financing cost has to be included in the cost of operations and ultimately will affect the cost customers have to pay for goods and services. This, of course, impacts the ability to compete in price aggressive markets.

There is always a demand for cash in a corporation and there are many ways it can be used. Every manager will have programs that are deemed important and will be viewed by that manager as being most worthy of being funded.

In the budgeting process, cash needs are generally forecast based on projected sales and the expenses required to support those sales. When there is a need for cash beyond normal cash inflows, debt is usually employed to fill the gap.

A particularly vexing challenge is deciding how to maximize cash use. GWR Research developed a system that allows a manager access to any level of cash he or she believes is needed but charges interest on funds that are not used efficiently. The definition of cash efficiency will vary from organization to organization and is expressed in a mathematical formula.

The key to a successful cash management program is to have a base level of cash available to managers for normal operations supplemented by a self-adjusting formula based on efficient cash use. The base operating level will automatically be increased or decreased based on the managers' efficient use of cash.

The GWR method was first used for a grocery chain that wanted to build a new milk plant in San Antonio, Texas but did not want to borrow money. The chief executive officer felt there was enough cash flow in the 120 stores to free up the money to build a milk plant.

A senior team had been working on developing a cash management system for a couple of years but hadn't come up with a system that could be implemented successfully. Most of the approaches centered on the frequent harvesting of cash from registers in the stores and sending the cash to the local banks. The corporate office would then collect the cash from the various banks. What made the system impractical was the inability to accurately predict the amount of money each store would request for the next day's operation. Even if cash were harvested hourly from the stores, the managers might request an amount equal to or greater the next day for store operations. Stores needed cash to buy local inventory and cash customers' checks. Store managers did not want to disappoint customers or be unable to purchase local inventory items when they were needed and in many cases requested ample amounts of cash to ensure they could serve their customers.

It occurred to me that corporate managers shouldn't be involved in managing the cash at the store level. I gave it some thought and proposed a system that treated money requested by store managers as a loan from the corporate office. We established the loan rate as the same as charged by a bank. Store managers were told they could withdraw as much as they felt they needed without any interest charge as long as the money was efficiently used. Efficient use meant that if all of the money requested above the established target for the store were converted to inventory or checks, there would be no interest charge. Formulas were developed that would adjust the cash withdrawal limit for each store based on efficient use of cash.

Each store's withdrawal and deposit history was analyzed and was the basis for setting withdrawal targets for the store managers. If a store requested more than the withdrawal target for the store and redeposited cash, this excess cash was considered inefficiently used and received a penalty or interest charge. These interest or penalty charges were considered part of the store's operating costs and affected store managers' annual bonuses.

This approach involved store managers in controlling cash throughout the system and focused on efficient use of cash. The system, once implemented, freed up the cash needed to build the milk plant.

Use Key Performance Indicators as Management Tools

Having performance indicators can help improve virtually any facet of your business and will provide a good tool to assess the efficient use of cash resources.

Determining the business area to be monitored and the type of indicator will vary with business type. For example, in retailing, customer satisfaction may be gauged by repeat visits by customers, frequency that merchandise is returned, and customer complaints. For airlines, customer satisfaction indicators might include lost luggage and on-time departure and arrival statistics.

Key performance indicators should provide a gauge of success in achieving internal goals as well as comparing performance with industry averages or industry leaders. Having a comparison to the industry prevents managers from becoming myopic when measuring results. Performance considered acceptable by an individual company but below the industry norm may be headed for trouble.

Some companies produce key performance indicator reports monthly and distribute them with financial reports to managers and senior staff. By combining key performance indicators with financial outcomes, a manager is able to get a clearer picture of what is working well and what needs attention.

For example, a financial report might show a profit level that is meeting expectations or that revenues are at expected levels. When viewing key volume and productivity reports, it may show that product sales volumes are higher than expected and that labor costs are below expectations. Here a manager looking at just the financial reports would assume everything was operating in an acceptable range and that significant improvements couldn't be made. By analyzing nonfinancial performance indicators such as products produced per labor hours used and revenue per product, a manager in the foregoing example might find that the products are being sold at lower than planned rates and the employee productivity reduced labor costs enough to offset lower revenue per unit sold.

This might cause a manager to ask why the products were sold at lower than planned rates. Further study might find a problem with marketing efforts, sales staff, or product quality. Follow-up actions might result in solutions that would allow unit rates to increase while maintaining sales volume resulting in increased revenues and profits.

It is a good idea to have operational managers report on key performance indicators in their area of responsibility on a regular basis. Monthly reporting is preferred but such reports should be required at least quarterly.

Key performance indicators might include the following:

1. Workforce performance indicators
    a. Payroll costs per full time employee equivalent
    b. Products produced per person hour
    c. Customers served per person hour
    d. Revenue per person hour
    e. Benefit costs per full time equivalent
    f. On the job injuries per month
    g. Employee payroll and benefit cost per product sold or customer served
2. Production division indicators
    a. Percentage of available machine time used
    b. Repair and maintenance hours as a percentage of available machine time
    c. Material waste per unit produced
    d. Defective products per 1,000 produced
3. Financial indicators
    a. Days in accounts receivable
    b. Interest cost or discounts lost due to late payment

    c.   Discounts received for early or timely payments

    d.   Days of material in inventory

    e.   Inventory turns per inventory payment cycle

4. Customer satisfaction indicators

    a.   Customer product returns per 1,000 products sold

    b.   Customer complaints per 1,000 customers

    c.   Customers served per person hour

    d.   Number of out-of-stock reports per product line

5. Sales and marketing indicators

    a.   Revenue per customer

    b.   Profit per customer

    c.   Market share

    d.   Sales per sales employee

    e.   Sales administration costs per customer

    f.   Advertising costs per customer

    g.   Advertising and marketing costs per product sold

This list of indicators can be expanded or customized to meet specific business needs.

Using key performance indicator reporting on a regular basis will provide useful information on actions that will improve the overall performance of any organization.

Conclusion

This chapter has focused on the impact marketing strategies can have on organizational resources. We have looked at organizational structures and alliances that provide efficient implementation of marketing strategies. We also provided suggestions on approaches to use internal cash flows for growth and a process to monitor the organization's resource efficiency.

CHAPTER 16

Putting It All Together

This chapter will focus on the steps we have discussed in the previous chapters and present a process to help the marketing strategist develop a vision and mission driven strategy and implement strategy driven tactics.

As we have said, developing a marketing strategy is similar to planning for a trip. To plan a trip, it is necessary to determine where you want to go but it is just as important to know where your trip will start. Knowing your starting point and desired destination can be described as the vision for the trip or for a marketing strategy.

The mission for the trip is more about the experience you hope to have as you complete the journey. This experience will be determined in part by the resources available to you including time, money, modes of transportation, and so forth. For a marketing strategy, the mission or the experience you hope to have is driven by the hoped for business outcome, usually expressed in financial terms and desired market position. These outcomes are also determined in part by the resources available to the organization.

To plan for a trip, you take the time to think about the time you will be travelling to your destination, the time you will stay, and the activities in which you will participate. This will require an assessment of your available resources and how they may be managed to allow you to enjoy the trip. This may mean that you would choose a less expensive mode of travel to be able to participate in more activities at the destination. This planning will also consider factors such as the weather, airline flight cancellations, and accommodation availability.

For a marketing strategist, the planning for the trip stage is similar to the situation analysis—taking stock of the competitive landscape, the market opportunities and challenges, the organization's resources and capabilities, and the outside forces that may affect the implementation of a strategy.

To assist in planning, it is helpful to have a process that provides pointers. These pointers can be reminders of items that need to be considered or tools that help the planner understand all of the facets of the task. In the following section, an approach is presented that uses the steps outlined throughout this book that can be used in assembling a sophisticated marketing strategy.

A Strategic Marketing Planning Tool

Over the years, the leading marketing and management thinkers have developed theories that look for answers as to why companies failed after enjoying a period of tremendous success.

Theodore Levitt attributed failures to the leaders of these companies being myopic and defining their business mission too narrowly. For example, railroad companies considering themselves as being in the railroad business rather than the transportation business were myopic and prevented them from entering into air transportation, shipping, and trucking.

Clayton Christensen developed the theories on disruptive innovations and suggested that, over time, industry-leading companies continued developing product enhancements that were driven by the most demanding and profitable customers. As a result, a significant portion of customers not wanting or needing all of the product enhancements were vulnerable to attack from new companies offering less expensive, "good enough" product alternatives.

W. Chan Kim and Renee Mauborgne developed theories suggesting that "blue oceans" of opportunities existed within the traditional competitive business environment. These blue oceans provide opportunities for new companies to enter the market in a way that is protected from existing market participants.

All three theories are correct and are overlapping. An industry leader that begins to lose market share to new market entrants may have defined the scope of business too narrowly, focused too much on the most profitable customers, or left identifiable market opportunities unidentified. In fact, it is probably a combination of all of these factors that causes a company to become stagnant and ultimately begin to fail.

Recognition of the need for a broader marketing strategic planning effort is the first step in developing an ongoing strategic marketing process that can keep a company at the leading edge of its industry.

This process begins with a situation analysis that assesses the state of the marketplace, the industry, and the strengths, weaknesses, opportunities, and threats that affect the company as well as its competition.

After the situation analysis, there should be an assessment of the vision of the company. Are there occurrences that would suggest that the company's vision is too narrow? In the newspaper industry, the occurrence of digital delivery of news and classified advertising might have suggested that newspapers were in the information distribution business.

Further, if newspapers had taken a different view of niche, free distribution news products, there might have been a realization that a good enough product was attracting their least profitable customers. This would be an indication that a market disruption was possible.

Finally, a Blue Ocean Strategy Canvas (Figure 16.1) might have revealed opportunities that resulted in new businesses such as online searchable classified ads. This could have been an opportunity for newspapers as well as companies like Craig's List.

Using all three of the theoretical approaches provides better insights and a grid can be developed to identify strategic actions for price, place, product, and promotion and assess the needed requirements for the workforce, cash requirements, operational procedures, and capital expenditures. This process can also identify potential gateways that can allow a transition from the current mode of operations to a new business scenario.

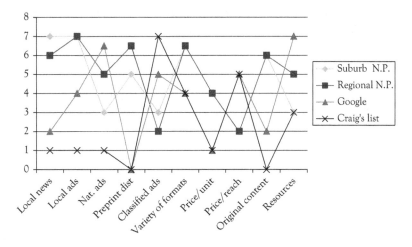

Figure 16.1 Blue Ocean Strategy Canvas

An Example

To demonstrate how to use this process, I will use a regional newspaper as the industry leader in a rapidly changing marketplace to develop a possible marketing strategy. The vision is to be the region's leading information source.

Situation Analysis Worksheet

Industry:

1. Changing to digital access
2. Old model of ad value changing
3. More focus on custom advertising
4. Print revenue losses not replaced by Internet revenues
5. Print and deliver model has high variable and fixed costs
6. Significant number of readers and advertisers prefer print and deliver model for news, advertising, and preprints
7. Consolidation or reduction of workforce due to technology
8. Technology is continuing to be more sophisticated and less expensive

Market:

1. Numerous suburban newspapers that have high readership in their community
2. Internet is increasingly the preferred choice to obtain news and information
3. Population and economic growth is highest in the suburbs
4. Suburbs attract younger professionals who are less likely to prefer printed newspaper

SWOT Analysis

1. Strengths: reputation, wide distribution network, corporate resources, local and regional news coverage
2. Weaknesses: print product cost structure, low penetration in markets with strong suburban newspapers

3. Opportunities: digital market growth, desire for relevant information, new technology developments and cost reductions, increase in availability of customized Internet application
4. Threats: competition with smaller, more productive staff, rapid growth of population and retailers in suburbs, decline in print audiences

Potential Disruptions

1. Low-cost cell phones with limited capabilities and no contracts
2. Digital preprints
3. Independent journalists covering specialty news and distributing digitally
4. Digital ad agencies to place ads for all formats

Marketing Mix Value Grid

A successful marketing effort requires the creation of value for a company, its customers, and its collaborators. The only way this value can be created is through the mix of the four marketing Ps. The mix that is successful provides a profit for the company and a product or service that is acceptable to a set of customers. The greatest creation of value to all concerned is based on the optimal value of the 4Ps used in concert. The Marketing Mix Grid (grid 1) provides an approach to identify the optimal marketing mix (see Table 16.1).

To find the Optimal marketing mix simply line up the horizontal and vertical squares leading to each of the four Ps. For example, to find the optimal Place to create customer value, squares 1C, 3C, and 5C would have to be addressed. To find the optimal Place to create value for the company, squares 1B, 4B, and 5B would have to be addressed. The location and logistics that addresses the requirements for the customer and company value creating squares combined yields the optimal Place (location and logistics) strategic component of the marketing mix and assures that the resulting Place strategy for creating customer value is in alignment with the Place strategy for creating value for the company. Repeating this for each of the four Ps determines the optimal value for each element of the marketing mix that assures alignment in creating value for the customer and the company. The resulting matrix provides the best strategy that supports company, customer, and collaborator success.

Table 16.1 Marketing Mix Value Grid—grid 1

	Price	Place	Product	Promotion
Price	Optimal Price	1B. Price charged fits with costs to get product to customer location	2b. Price charged provides needed mark up to cover costs and profit needs	3b. Price charged covers all marketing costs
Place	1c. Customer's price fits with the search time intensity customer is willing to expend	Optimal Place	4b. Location and logistics maximize ability to efficiently distribute product to customer	5b. Location and logistics ties with branding and communication efforts
Product	2c. Product is priced to fit customers budget and amount willingly paid for value received	3c. Location and logistics match customers' expectations for product acquisition	Optimal Product	6b. Product lends itself to promotion efforts that can support needed revenues and volumes
Promotion	4c. Promotion supports value indicated by price paid by customer	5c. Promotion utilizes location, and logistics are interpreted as customer benefits and are part of promotion efforts	6c. Product promotion focuses on customers' expectations of product doing the job they need done	Optimal Promotion

Note: Area above and to the right of diagonal arrow creates value for company, area to the left and below diagonal arrow creates value for customers and collaborators.

Source: Copyright GWR Research.

Company Value

The value for the company rests on its ability to capture the value created for the customer in the form of profits. The best approach to address the requirements for the company value creating squares (those above and to the right of the diagonal arrow) is to determine a clear understanding of the direct costs and the mark up provided by the price willingly paid by the customer for the products and services offered and the size of the market. This understanding provides the strategist with an estimate of the cash flows that will be available to sustain the organization.

A situation analysis that is part of the marketing plan regimen usually requires that an assessment of the customer base, competition, industry, and so forth take place before any marketing goals are set. This would be critical in determining potential price ranges, competition, and size of the market.

Once direct costs are understood then a break-even analysis can help determine the strategy used for fixed costs. This approach allows the potential cash flows that result from providing customer value to drive the nature of the strategy rather than a preconceived notion of how the organization should be developed that might have an emotional foundation.

Customer Value

Creating customer value is by providing products or services that fulfill a need and for which a customer is willing to pay a certain price and expend a certain amount of effort to acquire. To assess the appropriate customer value creating squares (those below and to the left of the diagonal arrow) a clear understanding of forces that cause customers to purchase a product or service. Here a set of Consumer Adoption Drivers developed by GWR Research and based on research studies by Gerald Zaltman and Nan Linn prove useful.

To determine the best approach to address the requirements for customer value creation squares, each square should be measured against the Consumer Adoption Drivers (CAD) shown in the following list.

The CAD list is as follows:

1. Group influence intensity: relates to peer pressure exerted on customers.
2. Perish ability: the length of time the product is deemed useful.
3. Psychological appeal: status associated with the product.
4. Price sensitivity: the need for the customer to budget for the purchase.
5. Relative price influence: the attractiveness of other products as a substitute when price is a consideration.
6. Frequency of purchase: the frequency with which the customer purchases the product.
7. Search time intensity: the amount of time invested in the search for the "right" product.

8. Tangible differentiability: physical differences between products.
9. Intangible differentiability: nonphysical differences between products (guarantees, relationships with company, branding etc.).
10. Technical complexity: the need for training before a customer can use the product. This may be a factor in determining the type of sales force that will be required.

For example, square 1C would be considered against each CAD. It might be that the product is frequently purchased and there may be several products easily attainable that could be used as a substitute. It might also be found that peer influence or psychological appeal plays an important decision in where the customer shops. These attributes along with other CAD attributes might impact the time and effort a customer is willing to locate the right product. This can help describe the location and logistics that will create the greatest overall value.

Usually the best approach to understanding the CADs for a potential market is to conduct focus groups or surveys of potential customers to determine the importance of each of the CADs as they relate to the proposed product or service. These measures can then be applied to each of the four Ps to determine the optimal characteristics for each of the 4 Ps to create value for the customer.

Collaborator Value

Collaborator value is best determined by providing a structure that allows the vendors, brokers, alliance members, and other contributors to benefit when the optimal value is created for the customer and company. This, in most cases requires an organization that can create value by providing benefit to the customer. For this reason having collaborators aligned with creating value for customers is most advantageous.

Strategy Worksheet

Based on the aforementioned series of analyses, a strategist can begin to develop a strategy spreadsheet for price, place, product, and promotion that are measured against the impact on the organization's workforce, cash requirements, operational procedures, and capital equipment requirements.

For our regional newspaper example and based on the previous analysis, strategies that might be considered are:

1. Product: Focus on local and regional news coverage, develop products for conversion of print products including digital preprints, develop customized news and information delivery capabilities and software applications. Develop classified free digital classified ads with a print upgrade.
2. Price: Low cost for all digital products and cost-based pricing for print products. Preprint delivery would be priced to compete with "marriage mail" products.
3. Place: Print products delivered with long-term plan to convert to digital delivery. Preprint delivery would be by news carrier or post office with long-term plan to convert to digital delivery.
4. Promotion: Emphasize local news and shopping information, original content, and classified ads with impact. For advertisers, emphasize low cost per reach.

Since each strategic move has implications for the organization, each of the strategies considered should be measured against the impact on the organization as shown in Table 16.2.

Table 16.2 Organizational impact chart

	Product	Price	Place	Promotion
Workforce	Content stringers, mixed with employees for content. Internal sales staff	High productivity for staff through technology	Outsource and contract for printing and distribution	Internal brand manager. Outsource ad campaigns
Cash requirements	Minimize fixed expenses for facilities and so on	Cash flows maximized	Distribution costs below revenues	Utilize efficient promotions but have constant market pressure
Op. procedures	High use of technology and outsourcing	High use of technology and outsourcing	High use of technology and outsourcing	High use of technology and outsourcing
Cap. equip. requirements	Outsource software development and lease equipment	Outsource software development and lease equipment	Outsource software development and lease equipment	Outsource software development and lease equipment

Source: Copyright GWR Research.

As a marketing strategy is developed, it is important to recognize that individual elements of the strategy do not stand alone. Price, place, product, and promotion are interconnected. Price can affect the image of the product and the organization and influence the nature of the promotion. Promotion can affect the price, the product, and the mode of distribution.

As each of the four Ps has an impact on the others, they have an impact on cash flow requirements, management systems, workforce requirements, and capital equipment.

At this point, the strategist has a pretty good feel for what is needed to begin considering tactics. The tactics will describe how each action and organizational implication will be addressed specifically.

For the development of tactics, a chart similar to the organizational impact chart can be developed. The tactics are specific actions that would be used for the execution of the strategy. An example of how a tactics chart might look is presented in Table 16.3. This chart covers planning, organizing, operating, and control procedures for the workforce, cash, operating procedures, and capital equipment.

After the completion of the charts, the plan can be fully developed with activities, time lines, and budgets.

Using the prior approach allows managers to document the phases to the development of a marketing strategy; ensure that each element of the situation analysis has been completed; the four Ps of strategy have been considered; and the planning, organizing, directing, and controlling components for the workforce, cash requirements, procedures, and equipment have been considered.

The approach allows the strategist to ensure that each element is considered and that the tactics are in concert with the overall strategy and they are in concert with each other.

Table 16.3 Marketing tactics planning chart

	Product	Price	Place	Promotion
Workforce plan	Content stringers, mixed with employees for content. Internal sales staff. Outsource printing	High productivity for staff through technology	Outsource and contract for distribution	Internal brand manager. Outsource ad campaigns
Workforce organization	Develop program to encourage stringers to find compelling local and regional stories. Internal sales staff structured by customer segment	Contractors are given a set price for articles. Sales force commissions are focused on achieving sales goals. Inability to meet sales goals results in reduced pay	Printing outsourced to quality printers based on bid process and guarantee of press time. Alternate printers would be available for overflows and emergencies. Distribution contractor bids for delivery area would be awarded based on rate and quality	Brand manager would find a mix of media to meet goals within prescribed budget
Workforce procedures	Develop standards of performance for contractors and employees	Develop standards of performance for contractors and employees	Develop standards of performance for contractors and employees	Develop standards of performance for contractors and employees
Workforce controls	Develop metrics to evaluate workforce productivity and success; for example, sales per person, articles per week, and so on	Develop metrics to evaluate workforce productivity and success; for example, sales per person, articles per week, and so on	Develop metrics to evaluate workforce productivity and success; for example, cost per page, cost per address delivered	Develop metrics to evaluate workforce productivity and success. New customers per promotion
Cash plan	Cash needed to cover operating costs, operating facilities, and capital expenditures	Use discounts for early payment and penalties for slow payments. Negotiate vendor payments that allow cash collections to cover payments	Long-term lease for offices. Purchase of central office if better use of cash	Production costs included in promo expense. Negotiate for media rates, use trade out if possible

(Continued)

Table 16.3 Marketing tactics planning chart (Continued)

	Product	Price	Place	Promotion
Cash organization	All receipts and vendor pmts made through central bank	All receipts and vendor pmts made through central bank	All receipts and vendor pmts made through central bank	All receipts and vendor pmts made through central bank
Cash procedures	Invoices approved by operating manager, submitted to ap for pmt. Lock box for customer pmts	Invoices approved by operating manager, submitted to ap for pmt. Lock box for customer pmts	Invoices approved by operating manager, submitted to ap for pmt. Lock box for customer pmts	Invoices approved by operating manager, submitted to ap for pmt. Lock box for customer pmts
Cash controls	Performance metrics—profit/unit, net cash flows, and so on	Metrics—markup/product, profit/unit, sales volume	Rev/sq. ft., cost/sq. ft., and so on. Cost/customer delivery versus rev/customer delivery	Sales volume change per dollar of media expenditure, surveys to measure impact
Systems plan	Financial and misreporting	Financial and misreporting	Financial and misreporting	Financial and misreporting
Systems organization	Departments prepare reports for management each month	Departments prepare reports for management each month	Departments prepare reports for management each month	Departments prepare reports for management each month
Systems procedures	Departments prepare reports for management each month	Departments prepare reports for management each month	Departments prepare reports for management each month	Departments prepare reports for management each month
Systems controls	Financial, mis-, and performance metrics reviewed each month	Financial, mis-, and performance metrics reviewed each month	Financial, mis-, and performance metrics reviewed each month	Financial, mis-, and performance metrics reviewed each month

Table 16.3 Marketing tactics planning chart (Continued)

Equipment plan	Lease major equipment, purchase small equipment	Lease major equipment, purchase small equipment	Lease major equipment, purchase small equipment	Lease major equipment, purchase small equipment
Equipment organization	By department	By department	By department	By department
Equipment procedures	Defined by department. Management and approved by senior management	Defined by department. Management and approved by senior management	Defined by department. Management and approved by senior management	Defined by department. Management and approved by senior management
Equipment controls	R&M costs versus revenue production, rev/fte, cost/unit	R&M costs versus revenue production, rev/fte, cost/unit	R&M costs versus revenue production, rev/fte, cost/unit	R&M costs versus revenue production or brand impact

Note: R&M = repair and maintenance.
Source: Copyright GWR Research.

Conclusion

The process described in this book allows managers to develop marketing strategies in a manner that is structured and underscores the interconnectedness of an organization's activities with the implementation of the strategy. The process lets a manager determine whether or not a strategy is in keeping with the organization's mission and whether it has a reasonable chance for success. Finally, the process requires a manager to analyze the impact of the strategy on the organization before implementation which, as a result, can reduce strategic mishaps.

References

Randazzo, G.W. *Manager's Guide to Building a Successful Business*. New York, NY: BEP, 2013.

Index